Copyright © 2023 Jane Stanley

All rights reserved.

Introduction
by Jane Stanley (neé Evers)

Bryan Grosvenor Evers was the middle son of Frank Percival (Percy) and Ellen Emily (Nellie, née Grosvenor) Evers. He was born on the 16th January 1912 and lived at Thicknall Rise, Hagley, Stourbridge, Worcestershire with his older brother Tony and younger brother Keith. Theirs was a happy childhood, enriched with many friends and an extended family of numerous cousins, uncles and aunts, many of whom lived nearby. He went to Packwood Haugh Prep School before starting at Rugby where his housemaster at Cotton was his uncle Claude Evers, one of Percy's younger brothers. Whilst at Rugby he joined the OTC, becoming Cadet Sergeant. After school Bryan joined the family firm of solicitors, Harward and Evers in Stourbridge, in general practice, also attending lectures in the Law faculty of Birmingham University. Much later, when the firm joined Higgs and Sons circa 1989/90, he remained as a consultant.

His interests were many and varied. He was President of the Stourbridge Rotary Club* in 1955/6 and President of both the Dudley Law Society and the West Midlands Coroners' Society. He was Coroner for North Worcestershire from 1947-1982 (following in his father's footsteps who had been Coroner 1921-1947) and he captained Stourbridge Rugby Football Club. After the war he was a founder member of the Old Comrades Association and regularly attended the annual Qatia Day Service in Worcester Cathedral. He camped and canoed until he was well into his seventies when arthritis restricted his mobility. More often than not he was accompanied by younger members of his family who were thrilled to be driving along with him, the roof of his car down, towing the trailer and canoes and being greeted by all and sundry as they sped along. Morris Minors were his favoured mode of transport and he prided himself on being able to keep them going until the mileometer reached the maximum of 100,000 miles whereupon it reverted back to 0! (* In 2009 the Stourbridge Rotary Club donated a tree dedicated to him at the National Memorial Arboretum in Staffordshire. It stands on Rotary Ridge amidst 25,000 trees in the 150- acre site).

Above all else Bryan was a gregarious family man with a genuine endless interest in others. He did not marry but was a wonderful uncle to his six nephews and nieces - known to them as Uncle B. Such was his endearing personality that people of all ages were drawn to him for he made everyone feel they mattered. To be in his company was fun, stimulating and a privilege. His imaginative culinary skills became legendary and immortalised by his homemade Malteser ice cream, a constant favourite; his dice game (Zap!) is still played by younger generations.

The annual Brothers' Binge, started after the war by Percy and his three surviving brothers Ernest, Guy and Claude was an excuse for the four of them to meet up. Bryan's generation continued this tradition when it evolved into the Evers Cousins' Reunion, held every two years, and to which wives and young adult members of the family were included as well - you were eligible once you had left school. In the 1960s it was held in London at the Garrick Club where Harold Abrahams (Chariots of Fire), married to Bryan's cousin Sybil, was a member and well over fifty members of the family attended. The tradition continued for another fifty years and it is hoped there will soon be another one!

On September 1st 1939 Germany invaded Poland; two days later, honouring their guarantee of Poland's borders, Great Britain and France declared war on Germany. Bryan was 27. Upon joining the Territorial Army early in 1939 he resigned from the Stourbridge Voluntary Fire Brigade and after attending the Royal Military College he gained his commission. In 1940, 2nd Lieutenant B. G. Evers, Service Number 89661, 53rd (Worcestershire Yeomanry) Anti-Tank Regiment Royal Artillery was deployed to France.

His account makes little of the severity of his injury sustained during the Dunkirk retreat when he was effectively given up for dead. His family was notified that he was KiA (killed in action) and a memorial service was held for him in the local church in Broome. One can only imagine their shock, relief and joy to receive, a while later, a letter written by him from a hospital in France. Whilst One Man's War describes in detail his time, it omits to say how he would unravel wool from his fellow compatriots' worn out socks and jerseys and knit 'new' ones for someone's birthday, or how he conjured cakes using carrot peel and apple cores to supplement food which may have arrived in their parcels. After the war he knitted and crocheted baby blankets to welcome new arrivals to the family. The October 1941 version of the Rugby School Meteor magazine stated that on Thursday July 31st a cricket match using stools as wickets and a tennis ball was played between the Rugby and Marlborough POW soldiers - Rugby scored 57 runs, Marlborough 33.

In 1948 the Regiment was reformed as the 300th Anti Tank Regiment (Worcestershire Yeomany) RA and Bryan was the Officer Commander of P and Q batteries in Kidderminster.

Bryan lived a full and active life until he died aged 96 on 26th April 2008. It is surely testimony to his enduring popularity and the high regard in which he was held by so many that well over 200 attended his Memorial Service.

He wrote other short books, including 'The Ghosts of Harvington Hall' but he did not want 'One Man's War' to be published whilst he was alive. Because of the increased interest in WW1 and events relating to that time engendered by the Centenary Commemorations in 2014, and because future generations will surely want to know more when they commemorate WW2 in 2039, it seems a fitting tribute to re-visit the story of the life of a POW as told by an inspirational and unforgettable man.

Foreword
by Michael Evers (nephew)

"See that chap over there? I'm sure he was in the bag with me". Up he'd get, over he'd go, tap the chap on the shoulder - a few moments of confusion and then...sudden enlightenment. Hands would be shaken and laughter would break out, and off they would go. "Do you remember the time when...?" "Did you hear about old so-and-so...?" "Whatever happened to what's his name...?"

I lived at Thicknall through the 50s and 60s and many were the times when Uncle Bryan, assorted nephews and nieces and others taking part in canoeing trips or camping holidays, (anywhere in the country), might be sheltering from the rain in a cafe or pub, and the scene described above would have taken place.

Bryan was 27 when the WW2 started, a young solicitor in Stourbridge, probably destined for a fairly conventional (although not humdrum) existence. The war changed all that. It was described to me how, very smartly dressed in his uniform, he came into the office on the outbreak of the war to say goodbye to everyone and how thrilled he was at the prospect of doing his bit for the his country. What happened to him you will read in this book. I was too young to remember him before the war, although I was very much aware of his existence and how he had come back from the dead. I was 8 years old on his return and clearly recall the first time I saw him; he was digging the garden with his shirt off, the very opposite of the poor, beaten up, old soldier one might have been expected.

Bryan was a Captain. Prisoners of War who were officers (and particularly British officers) were undoubtedly treated much better than other soldiers. Even allowing for this, what comes through in his book is how well conducted life in prison camp generally was. Friendships were easily made, even with his

German captors. Would that still happen now? Who knows?

Bryan's friendships lasted a long time. Reggie Williams Thomas and Derek Woodward lived in Worcestershire so it is not surprising that he continued to see plenty of them; however he also kept up with people whom he would never have met had it not been for the fact that they had been in prison together. I can remember visits to Thicknall made by Jumbo Burrough, Dick Tomes and Peter Conder and, on several occasions, by Vincent Hollom. Ernest Edelman does not get a mention in the book, but Bryan would continue to visit him at his home near Taunton in Somerset into the early years of this millennium. It was not to be expected that Bryan would be able to keep up with any of the Germans whom he met whilst in prison; however, but in the late 40s he took me to meet the Dutch lady Lies Goedkoop (I stayed with her and her parents in Amsterdam), Mademoiselle le Cornu in Lille and the Perronets in Noyelles Godault.

He was very keen on international relationships and, chiefly through Rotary, he would give hospitality to large numbers of young men from all over the world. He never bore any animosity towards the Germans and dozens of them stayed with him at Thicknall or at Bank House over the years. In particular I remember Norbert Westenberger from Mainz and Theo Krygier, whose son Marcus became one of Bryan's many Godchildren.

It is a strange thing to say, but I believe the five years Bryan spent in prison camp were the highlight of his whole life, not at the time maybe, but in retrospect. This is borne out by the words in the final paragraph of his book. He was a truly remarkable man.

ONE MAN'S WAR

There is a day in the year when the eels must go down to the Sargasso Sea, and come what may, no one can prevent them. On that day they spit upon their ease, their tranquillity, their tepid waters. Off they go over ploughed fields, pricked by the hedges and skinned by the stones, in search of the river that leads to the abyss.

> Wind, Sand and Stars,
>
> Antoine de Saint-Exupery,

BUT I ASSURE YOU, MY DEAR CHAP — I REALLY **AM** FATHER CHRISTMAS!

FOREWORD

This is a personal account of one man's individual reactions to events in wartime which happened only to him. They are a minute and un-important part of the experiences of millions in the Second World War, the totality of which makes up the history of an important episode of our time. It is perforce egocentric and recalls only the highlights of five years of life, the exciting rapids to be negotiated in the course of a generally quiet and sluggish river. The longueurs are now but thinly in the memory, and can only be hinted at. I have been asked to tell the story, so here it is, for what it is worth.

1939

The war engulfed me, as it did the rest of Europe two days later, on the 1st September 1939 when my regiment was called up with most of the Territorial Army, except the Anti-Aircraft Batteries which had already been mobilized.

I had joined the Territorial Army in February 1939, when I realised that war was inevitable, and that Hitler's appetite was insatiable and his word valueless. I had therefore reluctantly left the Stourbridge Voluntary Fire Brigade and was gazetted as a 2nd Lieutenant and posted to the Kidderminster Battery of the Oxfordshire and Worcestershire Yeomanry. Derek Woodward and Ernest Hollis joined at about the same time.

Some things were very strange. I had spent some years in the O.T.C. at school as an infantryman. I now had to learn as a cavalryman to wind puttees down from the top and not up from the bottom as in the infantry, and also to form fours in a new and complicated way as though we were still on horseback, which we were not. I never mastered this odd manoeuvre, and thank heavens we almost at once paraded and marched in threes not fours, and wore gaiters not puttees.

Our role had very recently been changed from Field Artillery with 18 pounder guns to an Anti-Tank Regiment with 2 pounders. This must have been much to the dismay of the old officers of the regiment, but it did mean that the "young officers" knew almost as much about the new role as anyone else. We spent much of our time doing gun drill, which was quite fun and competitive, and attending "Tactical Exercises without Troops". One conference was held at Haseley in the fine house of Lt. Col. A.J. Muirhead, the C.O. of the Regiment who was also Under Secretary of State for India. The party included The second Lord Birkenhead, Freddie, Charles Lyttelton whose father, Lord Cobham, was Under Secretary for War, Ronnie Cartland, M.P. for Kings Norton and one of Eden's men I think, and other officers of the Regiment. Joining us were two nephews of Winston Churchill. We also attended a camp at Trawsfynydd. It was terribly wet, and I learnt what an incredible degree of wetness was needed before it would be said to be "inclement" and worthy of a rum ration. Nevertheless we learnt to fire the guns - and kill some sheep - a lot more about tactics and moving and placing the guns, recovering bogged down vehicles, and generally getting to know each other.

Much however was soon changed, as the regiment had in March 1939 doubled in size and split to form the Worcestershire Yeomanry 53rd A/T Regiment R.A. and The Oxfordshire Yeomanry Regiment 63rd A/T Regiment R.A. Lt. Col. Bill Wiggin was our C.O. and I was posted on mobilization to 212 Battery at Kings Heath. It was there, in between spells of slit trench digging, that we heard on the radio Chamberlain's speech at midday on the 3rd September telling Britain that we were at war and "It is evil things that we are fighting against".

The expected air raids did not happen, but black-out regulations were strict. When I try to tell young people who, and now whose parents, do not remember the war, I tell them that on the 2nd September one could, standing on the top of Clent Hills, read the newspaper by the lights of the Black Country as one can now. As I was still sleeping at home at the time I was able, on the night of 3rd September on my return from Kings Heath, to walk up onto the hills and look out over Birmingham and the Black Country and see hardly a glimmer of light. This was symbolic of the severance of war time life from the life before it.

We were very untrained and we were also in the doubling up process, taking in new recruits whose abilities were quite unknown to us. One of the first things I did was to take my troop on a map reading exercise from our headquarters in Kings Heath. Anyone who had a civilian driving licence might be made a driver. As soon as we got outside the precincts my driver ran into a stationary tram, which was an inauspicious start, but there was little damage and we went on our way.

It was not long before we were moved to our training area, Wantage and the Berkshire Downs. I was billeted with the local miller; he and his wife were devout Methodists, teetotal, as I was at that time. They were extremely kind, and had a tennis court on which I played occasionally. There was also in the town a man named Sugden who was then a master at the local Grammar School, but he had taught me while he was a master at Rugby, and through him we had the run of the school fives courts, and I was initiated into the art of Eton Fives by Charles Lyttelton. We spent time in doing exercises on the Downs; I used an old Roman Camp as a ground for a game of "flags" or "French and English" by night. The men were all from Kings Heath area, and though very intelligent, some were not used to the dark. They enjoyed it too. Our time at Wantage was a happy one. The townspeople were all very good to us, including the Convent School, who provided much hospitality, as did the doctor and the town clerk whose wife was an artistic woman and a good photographer. Of him there is a story. One of the Battery Commanders, Dick Wiggin, was introduced to the Borough Surveyor, and told him how glad he was to meet him, as he had heard of him all his life. This was because of the limerick:

> "There once was a Town Clerk of Wantage,
> Who of a young girl took advantage,
> Said the Borough Surveyor,
> I'm afraid you must pay her,
> As you've altered the shape of her frontage".
> "Yes", said the Borough Surveyor,
> "I like the limerick myself,
> but my friend the Town Clerk,
> whose name is Fullalove,
> doesn't like it quite so much".

There were, as far as I was concerned, two interruptions to this quite happy period. The first was when we went to a firing camp at Lydd. It was bitterly cold, and the billets were damp, with paint peeling off the walls. More important was the fact that we all fired very badly and clearly showed our lack of training. Later, just after Christmas, which we had spent at home on embarkation leave, some of us went on a course on A/T gunnery at Lark Hill, and this was very inspiring. When I returned to the Regiment, which was only just before we embarked for France, Lt. Col. Medley, who, as I shall recount, had come as our new C.O., asked me about the course and how long it would take to train the gun crews. I said 3 weeks. The move to France intervened but on the

8th February we went to a firing camp at Calais and there all the shooting was greatly improved, particularly 212 Battery and my own troop. So my prophesy was more or less fulfilled. (Incidentally, this Calais episode was an eye opener, as we were billeted in the Caserne and it was indescribably filthy and it had to be cleaned and disinfected before we could settle into it).

While we were still at Wantage new plans were made for the regiment. It was to be reunited with the Oxfordshire Yeomanry to form a first and second line. 212 Battery was to go to the second line, and the first line was to be commanded by Col. Muirhead and embark with the 48th Division. Very soon after this announcement Col. Muirhead committed suicide, for reasons I do not know. All the officers attended the funeral and Ronnie Cartland and I and a party of men formed a guard of honour. We tried to recall our O.T.C. infantry training so as to make a reasonable show of drill and slow marching. No more was then heard of the reorganisation plan; had it gone through I suppose I might have spent all the war in Northern Ireland as the Oxfordshire Yeomanry did. Thus it was that we went abroad in the 48th Division among the first Territorials to do so; Lt. Col. Bill Wiggin had however been replaced on grounds of age by Lt. Col. E.J. Medley, a regular officer, and he soon made his mark on the Regiment.

France

We sailed from Southampton. I was orderly Officer of the ship, but thank heavens was not brought into action; we arrived without incident at Le Havre on 9th January 1940. The weather was bitterly cold, and we found the vehicles, which had been sent ahead of us, were in a terrible state, many of them having been frozen up and with burst engine blocks or radiators. Half our trucks were in fact towing others; there had been no issue of antifreeze, and the only defence against this weather was to empty the radiators. At last after nights at Yvetot and Blangy we arrived in our positions and found our billets in the Mines de Dourges near Noyelles Godault, not far from Douai. Almost at once we were put on an alert against a feared westward move by the Germans, and we spent much of the night, in a hard frost, clearing the guns of grease and setting the sights, and repacking the vehicles in the expectation of a move into Belgium. The alert was lifted before long and we settled in to our new surroundings.

Our vehicles and guns were on the premises of the local mine. The coal mines were then working and coal dust was everywhere; it was a very bleak looking place, set in a flat and uninteresting countryside with conical slag heaps dotted about. The accommodation was primitive, particularly the sanitation. When using the "cabinet" one felt inclined to use one's gas mask, and it was almost worse when the horse drawn cart came to clear the cabinet and spread the contents on the fields around. There was one bath in the village of Noyelles Godault, in the doctor's house; it was used about once a week and it ran out on to the gutter of the road, where it froze. There were layers of bathwater like rings of a tree, marking the weeks as they passed. There were showers in the mines which we were able to use from time to time. Soon after we arrived a large proportion of the Regiment went down with flu and very bad coughs which I was lucky to avoid. A remedy which was applied by the lady with whom we "messed" was to "cup" the patient; this involved the use of small glass cups into which some cotton wool soaked in methylated spirits was placed, and then lit. These were then applied to the chest, and a suction caused. To see someone with a number of these cups on his chest and back was rather comical; it may have done good, but it was to us an unusual treatment.

The welcome the local people gave us was warm and gracious, but as can be imagined there was much opportunity for misunderstanding, both of language and culture. For example our Battery Commander, Major Reggie William-Thomas, was spoken of by the troops as "the Major". Some French people hearing this thought he was "le Majeur", and on one occasion someone came up and asked that he should, as a matter of urgency, attend a woman in her confinement as the local doctor could not be found. "Majeur", apparently means "Medical Officer". I think the invitation was refused!

On one occasion, towards the end of our stay in this area, we decided to hold a dance in the local hall to thank the townspeople for their hospitality to all our troops. We therefore asked our men to invite the young girls of the area to this dance, for which we had hired a piano and got in food. We all turned up on the night, and awaited our guests. The only girl to arrive was the keeper of one of the "estaminets" whom we called the Merry Widow. Apparently we had committed a terrible social faux pas by asking the young girls without their mothers. Our French Liaison Officer had never warned us and the evening was a flop and a great disappointment to our troops. The Merry Widow however had a splendid evening!

We spent most of our time in practising with the guns, doing maintenance on the vehicles and going on exercises, but we also had from time to time to provide fatigue parties to help to build the pillboxes on the "Gort Line", an extension to the north of the Maginot Line. These were in an early state of construction, much smaller in fact than the official maps showed, and there must have been some sabotage by Fifth Columnists, since later on we found a concrete mixer concreted in to interfere with the line of sight from one, at least, of the pillboxes.

We also had some sporting activity. We played local football teams, composed largely of Polish mineworkers, and we also held the Regimental Sports, which went well. I must have had something to do with the organisation, as I recall enlisting the services of the "Divisional Mobile Bath Unit", and they were delighted to be noticed, since this was the only occasion on which they had had to do anything in the whole of the time they had been in France.

We were fairly civilised with a good officers' mess and reasonable food, though the Battery Captain, whom I succeeded, tried to introduce nettles and Healthy Life Biscuits into the diet; the troops thought they were being poisoned!

The Battery Commander maintained the cavalry traditions by buying a charger on which he rode on available occasions to the admiration, no doubt, or possibly amusement, of the locals. Unfortunately it could not come with us into battle.

One of my pleasant recollections is of another alert in April. In order to be near the border, and so make a quick move into Belgium if she were attacked, we drove out of the Noyelles Godault area to Flines les Raches where we waited for orders to advance into Belgium. Since it was staying neutral, Belgium would not, unless attacked, allow troops to cross the frontier, and anyone who did was interned.

Flines was a very grateful contrast to the mining area we had been in; it was a wooded countryside and the poplars with the light green of spring raised ones spirits and the air seemed so fresh after the coal- ridden air of the mines. But the red alert was withdrawn after some days and we returned sadly to Noyelles; the trial run proved most useful a month later. On our return we felt that the villagers were sorry to see us come; naturally they were trying to re-establish their lives and grudged the resumption of our occupation. The warmth of their previous welcome and kindness was this time partly withheld.

Two things about this period came to mind. During the very cold days of the winter we went on an exercise in the direction of Arras. On the flat fields we came across great holes in the ground which reminded me of the crownings of the Black Country, the falling in of coal or fireclay workings, leaving a cavity. We were told that it was the Hindenburg line which, after 23 years or so, was at last collapsing in the freezing weather. Later on I went to look at Vimy Ridge and saw the trenches of the opposing armies of the First World War, unbelievably close together. What a ghastly business that war was!

The other event was a display of French tanks and armoured vehicles in the direction of Cambrai. We were not at all impressed, as the vehicles seemed old and primitive and did not perform well. On the way back I made a diversion through fields golden with buttercups to Vendegies where in a small cemetery, beautifully tended as usual, was the grave of my uncle Lance Evers, who died
a few days before the end of the First World War. Somehow, in retrospect, this seemed an appropriate encounter.

So we moved into May. Reggie Williams-Thomas was due to go on home leave and I, as now the Battery Captain, would be in charge of the Battery. Ronnie Cartland, who was O.C. 209 Battery, and I were planning a big exercise together while Reggie was away. In fact Reg and I went to dinner in Ronnie's Mess on the 9th May and discussed events. Ronnie was certain that Neville Chamberlain must go, and I think was being urged by Lt. Col. Medley to go back to the House of

Commons to state his views in a secret debate. We asked him who was to take Chamberlain's place. He seemed uncertain and was not in favour of Churchill as he thought he was bad at choosing the people who were to work with him. As usual it was a very stimulating discussion.

We returned to our billets and noticed some unexpected activity, and we got into trouble for showing too much light on our vehicle. However we went to bed as usual, thinking more of a happy and interesting evening than the prospects for the morrow. We had not long to wait, since after two or three hours of sleep we woke to the sound of anti-aircraft fire. This sound was not too unusual, as raids had happened before, but they were reconnaissance or leaflet raids only. On this occasion however the fire was prolonged, and we heard explosions; from the window I could see planes with bombs falling from them. We received our orders, packed and said goodbye as best we could, and the Battery set off for the Belgian Frontier which we crossed at 3.p.m.

Belgium and Back Again

The role of the Regiment on this forward movement was to guard the route of the 48th Division as it moved up to the river Dyle, south of Brussels, the defensive line agreed with Belgium and our allies. We had 16 Bren guns per Battery and these were spread out along the 70 miles of the line of march to give some protection against low flying aircraft. We claimed six enemy aircraft brought down, with some casualties on our part. Our Battery was to cover the most forward part of the route, and we moved over the border immediately after the Divisional Cavalry and were welcomed by cheering Belgian crowds who threw food to us. We adopted, as we advanced, Queen Mary's circular wave of the hand to the enthusiastic population.

We arrived at our position at about 2.a.m. and settled in. The Officers' billets, which we chose at random, were a large chateau whose owner was fleeing to the West. Before he left he gave us the key to his wine cellar and urged us to drink as much as possible so that the Germans would not get it. This, with a bath and beautiful beds, was too good to last; Divisional H.Q. took it over the next day and we were sent to find a humble shelter for the next night.

By that time 212 Battery had been attached to the 2nd Div. A/T Regiment, and I remember that as we took up positions on the right of the British line we thought it would be well to make contact with the French on our right, and incidentally found a large gap in the infantry lines between the British and French, which we reported. Reggie Williams-Thomas and I found our opposite numbers on the French side. The French Battery Commander had a white beard and seemed to me very ancient. I remember him saying about Reggie, "Il est un enfant". We had little confidence in the security of our right flank, and by morning they had gone.

Then began a series of withdrawals which the breakthrough of the Germans at Sedan made necessary to secure our lines of communications to the Channel ports. As far as we were concerned our only contact with the Germans was when they dropped bombs or dive-bombed us, and we tried to beat them off, forlornly, with our Bren guns. I remember our first withdrawal when I found myself with the B. Echelon (service vehicles) in a Divisional Column led by a Staff Captain G3 who seemed quite unable to find his way to our next position. The maps of the area were terrible, and we had to move by night; if we were caught on the move in daylight we should have been dive-bombed to destruction. After being taken in the wrong direction a number of times I took my party off on a frolic of my own, going largely by compass; we arrived safely, but I found a considerable following of other units tacked on at the rear! I do not know what happened to the rest of the column. Other memories were the sight of the Lion of Waterloo perched on its mound; getting loaded up with stores from a Naafi which was being abandoned; another night withdrawal after many sleepless nights when the drivers went to sleep as soon as there was any hold up, and I spent the night going up and down the column, on a motor bike, waking them up, fearing what would happen if dawn came upon a sleeping column. There was the occasion too when I was with the service vehicles and men, separated from the main part of the Battery, attached to another division, on another part of the front, and told to find billets for the night. I found a farm for the troops and then a room with a bed in it for our French interpreter, Bob Chauvet and myself. I won the toss for the bed and I got in and went quickly to sleep, the first bed after more than a week's near sleeplessness. I never thought that I should see Reggie and Peter Dixon and the others again, at any rate south of the Channel, when suddenly I was woken up by a voice saying "Est ce que possible dormir ici?" to which I replied, "Yes Reg, come along in". He had chosen that farm of all others in that part of France to find somewhere for the night. What joy! How true are the unlikely stories in "War and Peace" and "Dr. Zhivago" of the bumping into friends and acquaintances in unexpected places on so large a zone of battle!

The next day was spent in trying to find rations and then we had orders to move by night through Poperinghe to behind a line of canals encircling Dunkirk and then, apparently to Dunkirk. We made our slow way along with drivers falling asleep at the wheel at every stop, and we were led down towards the town of Poperinghe. It was on fire and impassable, and I went in to reconnoitre a circuitous route through the small streets on the outskirts. I had heard of Poperinghe for many years, linked as it was with Tubby Clayton's Toe Hand Upper Room of the First World War, but here was an eerie and abandoned ruin of a town, many buildings ablaze and likely to come down at any time, fire hoses lying on the streets and explosions occurring throughout the town, empty and forlorn. At last we got through and stopped, and to our joy Peter Dixon turned up with the rest of the stragglers. Our column by that time was looking most peculiar. The vehicles were filled to the brim, not only with the Battery's equipment, spares etc. but also with an immense amount of Naafi stuff which we were loath to leave to the Germans - 6 dozen bottles of whisky, about 30,000 cigarettes and masses of chocolate. In the personnel carrying vehicles was an odd assortment of people collected en route, infantry mostly, making their way back - footsore, despondent and exhausted - towards Dunkirk. During this period of continual withdrawal, being separated from the Battery and rejoining it - lasting nearly three weeks - we saw very sad sights; civilians were moving westward with mattresses on the tops of their cars with all their goods inside; the poorer pushed everything on a cart or wheelbarrow; and I saw one young man pushing his father or grandfather and some chattels too, on a wheelbarrow; then there were the animals, some cows lying dead and bloated on their backs and others in agony because they had not been milked when their owners had fled; always there was fear on the faces of the civilians as they filled the roads and blocked our paths.

We came to a stop at a crossroads at Oost Cappell; the traffic, bound for Dunkirk, came flowing past, but it seemed doubtful if we should reach the beaches, and still more doubtful if we should manage to get home from there. However, ever optimistic, I put on my service dress and, fortunately, a good pair of boots. We waited for orders.

As we wanted to know how best to reach Dunkirk I was sent off on a motor cycle to make a reconnaissance. The traffic on the road seemed by then to have died down a bit, and in spite of rumours that we were cut off from Dunkirk I started off via Rexpoede. It was not long before the traffic thickened up - British, French and Belgian vehicles all head to tail. If a German plane came over, the column stopped and the drivers and men made for the ditches along the road with abject fear on their faces. I struggled on until it became clear that I could make no further headway, so I set out along a track, marked on the map, to the west. This began to peter out, so I stopped at a farm to find out if there was a way through or not. As I started to enquire, the sound of bullets around became disturbing and I gathered that the road through was a bad one, and that I should probably encounter the Germans not far away. So I turned about, found a road going in an easterly direction, and made my way back towards Rexpoede. On the way I came upon a troop of 25 pounder guns shooting up, so I was told, some enemy tanks over open sights; I hastened on to get back to the Battery, as it was clear that the only way to get to Dunkirk was by an easterly route.

When I got to Rexpoede I found crowds of French soldiers crowding round a tank. At the time I thought it was one of ours, but later I realised it was the collecting point for French prisoners. I found it was impossible to get along at all with the motor cycle, and so got on to a civilian bicycle, much too small for me, and made some progress in this peculiar style. At one part of Rexpoede there were two ammunition lorries on fire, exploding happily on either side of the road. Between these two I pedalled, and when I got back to the Battery I must have been an odd sight with the tyres punctured and the handlebars twisted. On the way I had seen one of our guns without any crew. The infantry seemed to have gone, and all this I reported. Part of the Battery and B Echelon had been sent by the eastern road to Dunkirk, leaving one troop only. I was then sent down, with a truck and driver, to see where the infantry was. We went first to Rexpoede where the fire was by now in good progress. I wanted to see whether there was any sign of infantry on the other side of the fire. I went round some buildings to look, but could only see some men making across the field.

I then went round close to the fire, and as I turned round some buildings I found a man in dark blue beckoning me on. I went up towards him, when I saw he was standing on a tank with a black cross very clearly marked on it. I thought discretion was the better part of valour, and ran as quickly as I could back to my truck. There were other people the tank had to think about, and nobody gave me one in the back as I rather expected. But when I arrived back I found the Major's fine truck had got peppered with mortar fire, and the driver was wounded in the ankle. I started to drive, but found it quite impossible, as the steering had completely gone. We had to find another truck, and fortunately the first we tried, a 15 cwt. Morris, was unharmed and in it we got back to the crossroads. By then it was clear that all the British Infantry had left the road and there seemed to be nobody else there at all.

In the meantime an artillery colonel had come up with two or three scout carriers. The crossroads where we were seemed an important junction, and one to be held. I offered to go back and try to scupper the tank near Rexpoede, and indeed obtained volunteers for the job, but it was thought unwise in the circumstances. Not long after, Peter was sent to Divisional H.Q. to give them particulars and bring back orders.

How hard it is to remember events consecutively! So many things were humming on the brain at the same time that it became hard and unreceptive, I suppose, but thereby able to work more quickly. There cannot, anyway, have been much gap in time before the enemy came close enough to put occasional bullets over, and then mortar. Meanwhile a staff captain from Divisional H.Q. came up and told us we must hold the crossroad, which we proposed to do with two guns and the carriers. By 9 p.m. enemy tanks were approaching, but were held up for the time being by grenades and an "antiquated" Frenchman with a prehistoric rifle.

I suppose it all happened very quickly, and indeed it does not seem long before we were throwing grenades around houses, having grenades thrown at us, and getting machine-gunned. Then we heard sounds of a tank approaching, and it soon moved around a house not more than 30 or 40 yards from the gun. The crew worked well and let off a number of shots, but the tank came on towards us, and I suppose six shots had been put into the tank before it came to rest not very far from us. I remember there was a man clothed in blue in agony on top, and the tank itself was clearly on fire inside. As it had come round the corner towards us, dark and menacing, it was an evil foe to be destroyed, but when the man jumped out all was changed; he was human, one of us, to be saved if possible.

And then mortar fire was brought to bear in earnest. The No.1 of the gun told me the No.3 had got hurt, and he wanted a relief. I took the seat temporarily myself, until a relief could be brought up. What happened after that I do not know; I had left the gun I think with the intention of moving it but got a bit of something in the back and I remember walking to a house nearby, used as a first aid post, and slumped down. I thought it was the end. There was no fear, and it all seemed quite natural, nothing more.

Imprisonment and Hospital

Occasionally I had momentary consciousness; the doctor cheering his patients, for reasons I afterwards knew; and at one time he said that we had been so successful at the outset and had got over-confident. I also remember him saying, "I do not know what to do with this captain, he is no good," and I also remember trying to impress him with my view that I was not going to peg out just then, but speech and movement were beyond me. Later there was a renewal of mortar attack, and the doctor said it was about time to leave before it was too late. Then I recall Sergeant Crocker trying to get me along with him. No doubt he was wounded too, and it was fine of him to risk his chances by worrying with me, when, as I now think probable, I was more or less given up for dead. I remember him telling someone, presumably the doctor, that he wanted to stay with me, and it was not until I had endeavoured to move with his assistance and had failed to energize a muscle, and until I had somehow ordered him to go with my good wishes, that he left.

The next thing I remember is waking up in the dark after a long and refreshing period of unconsciousness. There was nobody about; I called out in French and English with no result. The only inhabitant seemed to be a distressed Alsatian dog which prowled about the empty house like some lost spirit haunting the scene of its earthly life. It was quite an eerie affair.

After some time - my memory of these events and of the lapses of time is very hazy - I took stock. At any rate I was alive, and could move. My clothes were wringing wet, with sweat I suppose, so much so that my handkerchief in my pocket was soaked. I found I could sit up, and then somehow managed to stand and walk about. My desire was, of course, an intense one for self-preservation, and without much thought I went straight out of the back door and walked across the garden in the direction of Dunkirk, with the forlorn hope of finding an intact truck and driving hell for leather through any lines there might be. It was only an ephemeral freedom, however, for no sooner had I got towards the gate into the road than some Germans came round the corner of a building. I had a moment of triumph when I realised that they were more frightened than I was. I must have been a ghastly sight, white as a sheet and half clothed, slouching towards them all bent sideways, and as for me I was by then beyond fear. They shouted something about "Englander Tommy" and being unarmed and unable to do more than walk extremely slowly, I had to surrender.

I made some notes a few months later, somewhat influenced by the fact that they would be inspected from time to time by German censors but fresher than any tales I can tell now.

> "I explained in French - it is funny how I tried to talk French to the Germans, when English would have quite as good a result - but, I imagine, without impressing the six or eight Germans, that I was a British Officer. In any case they took me, and when they realised I was wounded, with some care, to the other side of the crossroads, that is to a cottage close to where we had been throwing our grenades.
>
> Being conducted into a German stronghold should, I suppose, have struck terror into my heart, and I should retain a vivid recollection of it. The presence of Germans, their field grey uniform and their

speech had, of course, seemed strange to start with, but I suppose that the whole affair had been so extraordinary and surprising that most of my faculties of perception were dulled. However that may be, the next thing I well remember is the miserable hovel where the German Regimental Aid Post was. It must by that time have been nearly 1 o'clock German time - 12 midnight by British time - and quite dark. The cottage was the usual French type with a table in the centre of the room and a stove jutting out into the centre. I remember sitting for the hours of the night, still in my soaking clothes but wrapped in a French overcoat, while at another corner of the room sat the French inhabitant, dirty, swarthy and spitting, while in the middle of the room a rather hard but efficient doctor bandaged up Germans and British alike with care and speed. Some of the British were pretty badly knocked about, and one in a way I hate to remember, and there was a good deal of groaning during the night which made sleep impossible. The thing I wanted most of all was a drink, warm and sweet, and in the end I managed to get this from the Frenchman, both for myself and some of the men, but he did not want the Germans to see what was happening. I also, when morning came, was able to persuade the Germans to allow me to totter to the place where all my things were, so as to obtain some whisky from my haversack. This certainly put new heart into the wounded, and the

Germans rather liked it too. The excursion also enabled me to see how the land lay, and I was interested to see that just outside there was a tank which had been part of the toll we indirectly took. In the morning there were quite a lot of shots, and I was told that my friends had come back to fetch me and were all dead. I was more worried by this than anything.

I do not know what the hour was when we moved to the German C.C.S. I suppose it was the afternoon. I remember that before I left I gave the Germans some whisky and thanked them for what they had done. They were really extremely pleasant, said that the war was over for me and that they would be in London in a month. I replied that the war would last ten years. It was a gruelling journey to the German C.C.S. I found it quite impossible to breathe when lying down flat, and there was no headroom to do anything else. However, I find one can bear all things, and indeed I did manage to look out of the window a bit, but it was pretty grim.

The road was terrible, and the ambulance, French, I think, seemed to have no springs either in its chassis or the bunks. However we got to the C.C.S. which was a farm somewhere behind Wormhoudt. One thing which struck me forcibly was the speed with which the blown bridges had been replaced by the Germans, though the crossing of the wooden affairs was the most painful part of my illness."

Incidentally the second tank which I saw was one which had been shot up after I was wounded.

In the C.C.S. (Casualty Clearing Station) I was interrogated in a perfunctory way. No doubt the Germans had all the information they needed, and did not proceed beyond the usual questions and the permitted answers. I was then allowed into a room with a bed, and after examination was allowed to go to sleep wrapped in the French Overcoat. How long I slept I do not know, but I awoke to the realisation of the position, and to the hopelessness, empty of purpose, which lay ahead. The Germans here were quite friendly. They enjoyed the whisky so much that I did not see it again, but that was no matter. In the afternoon I was taken again in an ambulance to Boulogne, and to a British hospital there. Here I met Major Laust, a Harley Street specialist I think, who looked me over, a Col. Harvey and a Padre Smith. I gathered from them that the food situation was very serious as the Germans had outrun their supplies. Major de Sallis and Captain Carter were the only patients in the room, both badly knocked about. It seemed that the piece of metal had collapsed my left lung, and I am now told - I am glad I did not know at the time - that it had lodged in my heart.

On the next day, 1st June, I was moved to Camiers near Le Touquet - another bumpy and uncomfortable drive. The hospital there was the British base hospital, a long white sanatorium of concrete and glass, collecting all the sun and looking out over green grass and the dunes to the sea. We were spared the clarity of air which would have enabled us to see England; there was just the blue sea and not a ship upon it.

We were there over 4 weeks. One of the first people I met there was Vincent Hollom, with whom I stayed for most of the rest of our prison life. He had been captured at Calais. There were several Specialists in the hospital, including Major Tucker, an international rugger player, and a Padre named Grundy who kept up our spirits with unlikely stories. There was also the M.O. of a Warwickshire Battalion named Crooks, who started planning, with me, to attempt an escape by boat. The idea was that as he had access to the wood workshops of the hospital he should build a canoe and we should cross to England in it. In those conditions one has wild ideas which keep up one's spirits, but this one had no future. In any case he was discovered before he had got far with the canoe building; he said he was making a coffin! Anyway the nights were moonlit and the winds contrary. It was good to have something to keep our minds off the immediate conditions and the prospects of what might lie ahead.

In a way those were weeks of tranquillity. We could hear sounds of battle in the distance and we had rumours of counter attacks and bombing of the German lines of communications to explain the poor rations, but apart from that it was a life of ease. My bed was between those of Charles and Donald Norris, brothers in the Gloucestershire Regiment. Donald was married to Mary, who had been a Chamberlain and her mother was the sister of my partner's wife, Enid Playne. Later in prison he died of appendicitis, a sad and unexpected end, no doubt contributed to by our diet and conditions. To start with I used to stay in bed until lunch and then got up to bask in the glorious sun. Much time was spent in sleep making up for long hours on the move. There were a few books to read. The one preoccupation was food; we were really hungry. The worst day was one in which we had two half rounds of bread for breakfast, a teacupful of soup, very thin, for lunch and 2 slices of cheese and 2 biscuits at tea time. Sometimes we had a pudding made of biscuits, and towards the end we managed to get white bread and butter, which made all the difference. Even so, in spite of shrimps somehow acquired and carefully measured out on a Sunday, we did not have enough to increase in strength after our various wounds. It was all put down to the fact that the R.A.F. was continually bombing the German ration columns and it was very hard not to think of food much of the time; in particular I craved for chocolate. I was thankful that I did not smoke; those whose cravings included cigarettes were in far worse case.

In the early days my breathing was very difficult, and I could not sleep on my side. When I got up I could do exercises which I devised to expand the collapsed lung and it quickly improved. The day then became a leisurely one; I got up fairly early and washed and every other day I shaved with a borrowed razor. I then had breakfast back in bed and waited for the doctors and slept until lunch to avoid thinking about food. After lunch at 12pm I got up and basked in the sun and read Mansfield Park, Old Curiosity Shop and Old Wives Tale, sometimes strolling about as much as I could. Then came tea, and a chat with some of the others, and back to bed. We passed our time fairly happily, talking of the past, thinking of the future. But the void inside us was not only from lack of food.

One diversion was the spate of rumours which were part of the stuff of a kriegies (short for Kriegsgefaugene, prisoner of war) life. They were called latrinograms in the more settled camps, because the latrines, whether urinals or banks of seats with little division, were meeting grounds for men from different parts of the camp and a scene for gossip. Most of the rumours were false, but in Camiers, some of those brought in by the French workers who tended the chugging diesel engine that provided the water and electric light - the bane of the patients who were on top of it - were true. They told us of the fall of France and the entry of Italy into the war, though they also said that Turkey was in the war, and that Turkey and Russia had entered German Poland, that America was in the war and so on. But for almost a fortnight we did hear gunfire to the south and out to sea, and we thought we noticed a thinning of the German guards from which we speculated on a second British Expeditionary Force backed by rumours of a landing of Canadians at Dunkirk and Boulogne.

Journey to Laufen

On June 28th, about a month after my capture, we were told that two officers had escaped and we must move, and the German M.O. came round to see who was fit to go. The English doctors urged that I should not be moved, but the German doctor would have none of this, claiming we were all going to be transported by truck to a convalescent home probably near Brussels. So next day, after farewells to doctors, orderlies and friends, we climbed into the bus and set off into the blue. Our first stop was at Hesdin, a filthy barracks where we had to sleep on bare boards but we got some stew and some white bread butter and sardines from a civilian.

On the 30th I noted:

"We moved, not too early, to Lille. On the way we, in our bus, overtook a number of troops on the march. They were nearly all French and Belgian; it was the first time I had seen them march and I was astounded at their slovenliness. Poor chaps, they had been marching for days, and one must not be critical".

In Lille we were taken to the arena and I noted:

"A barracks of unmentionable horror.

"Picture a few acres of ground with some buildings of large size scattered about in it, and in the middle a rectangle filled with guns of all sizes and descriptions from French 25mms to 6" howitzers. It was depressing merely to see the weapons the Germans had captured. But where we were expected to sleep was more than depressing. The floor was covered with straw in amongst which were eggshells, bits of bread, old wine bottles - and other nameless things. We cleaned the place as best we could, put down our gas capes to cover the remainder and in fact slept fairly well, in spite of the cold and the flies and the smell. Perhaps it was the outside of the buildings which was the worst part of it - I will not describe it, merely saying that there were at least 2000 men constantly moving through and there were no sanitary conveniences of any kind".

To get one's food one had to walk past a large pile of human excrement from which rose a sickly sweet smell, unforgettable.

In contrast with the foul conditions was the kindness of the civilians. The camp, flanked by railings, fronted a road, and French men and women came up and talked to us there. They gave us tea and various things to eat, and brought what they were able. One lady took my name and address and said she would write home via the Red Cross, and this she must have done. There was no kindness too great for them, and it is still a pleasant memory. We were begging almost without shame, though one wondered at the generosity of those who must have known that they would be facing a long period of deprivation themselves.

Perhaps the best part was just talking to outsiders. The French women said our defeat was entirely the fault of the French; their men, they said were not the stuff they had been, and I think they thought more of us than of their own countrymen.

Rumours multiplied. There was one, very much substantiated, that Calais had been recaptured and that motorised troops were within 10 kilometres of Lille. More possible, and many times repeated, was that 40,000 Germans had perished on an attempted landing in England, and their charred bodies were being washed up on the north coast of France. I am told that there were persistent rumours in England to the same effect.

Lille remains with me for three other events. The camp was filled with troops, French and English. Those of us who were wounded were to be taken by truck on our next stage, but the rest had to march. I remember it well; the French came out first, all sorts - Algerians, and Moroccans, black and white, in khaki and the French blue, with kepis and tin helmets, a cosmopolitan crew. But they marched as raggedly as tired men can and perhaps the French who practise the "broken step" are best at it. And then, at the rear, came our British troops, all in step singing a song and as proud as could be, and at a brisk pace. What a contrast! One of the French Officers who was standing with us was so impressed that he came to attention and saluted. It must have had as great effect on the people of Lille as it had on us.

The second was a sweet yet sad vignette. I saw two Moroccans lying down under a bit of an awning stretched from a gun wheel. They were eating their food quietly on their own, and among all this filth and with all the wrack of war around them, they had, between them, a vase with two roses in it. How or why they had got them I do not know, but it was a memorable and almost pathetically incongruous sight.

It was at Lille too that I heard of the death of Ronnie Cartland, shot I was told through the head, as he stood up out of a ditch to surrender the men he had with him. It was very distressing news; his dedication and energy and Christian convictions were infectious and he was a great loss to us all, not least to Britain which would have had great need of his services in Government if he had survived. But he would have hated being a prisoner - and indeed feared that he was on Hitler's black list and would have paid for his outspoken attacks on the Nazi Regime.

And so we left Lille, which I had seen before and after the battle. It had become a dead city, lacking all the gaiety it had once had but showing a kindness and generosity I had never seen and shall never forget.

The next port of call was Tournai gaol; I was in cell No.14 I think. It was fairly comfortable and clean and what was best of all we had a cold shower, the first time we had washed so well for over a month. We had bread, and rice for tea - no chance here of making contact with the civilians.

The following day was for me a hard one. It had been promised that we, the hospital cases, would be transported all the way into Germany, but in Tournai I was told that there was no transport for me. The most exercise I had taken since being wounded was an amble of about 1/4 mile round the hospital, but now I had to march about 15 miles from Tournai to Renaix. It was, fortunately, fairly flat, but I would never have believed I could do it; we have far more resources than we realise. Blisters and a pain in my side were the only unpleasant results. Against this can be set the goodness of the populace. Being at the back of the column I had no benefit from this, but in the front the French troops were plied with food etc. The guards too were forbearing, though the warning given to us by the Germans that if anyone tried to escape his friends would be shot did deter any attempt to slip away from the column. Certainly shots were heard from time to time.

The chief feature of the march was the singing of the Frenchmen. One in particular had an enormous voice which he exercised nearly all the way with good songs, e.g. "Il est coccu, le chef de gare". We put a brave face on things as we marched through the villages. I recall noticing, as we travelled through the Low Countries, that the countryside in those early July days was red with poppies, as had been the fields of Flanders 25 years before.

From Renaix, where I see I wrote home, to Ninove, and then again by truck via Alost and St. Nicholas to Locheran. In Ninove we were met by an American nurse who promised to write home and say she had seen us. Then on again by car to Moerbeke and on to a comical train journey. First we were in an open truck, and then a 3rd class compartment was put on for officers. The train ran through most fertile country, my first sight of Holland. The train was eccentric; the hedges lashed us while we were in the open trucks but once we went up the main street of a village where the population awaited us, pressing food upon us, sandwiches, salads, fruit and even bottles of milk. At last we got to the Rhine at Waalsorden, and embarked on the Konigin Emma.

My notes written in our first permanent prison camp now have a long gap. Though they were repetitive and had an eye to likely inspection by the Germans - they are marked "Gepruft" - they do now remind me of very many things I have quite forgotten. My story of the next stage without such notes is therefore of something recalled more than

40 years later. Very few incidents which still remain are now recoverable to my memory.

The Konigin Emma was a small river steamer, and in that we plodded up the Rhine, through the flat lands of Holland to Doordrecht and next on to Emmerich. It was hopelessly overcrowded; we slept where we could on the bare boards; I was lucky, in that I had brought with me one of the blankets from the hospital, thinking I was more entitled to it than the Germans. The most serious feature of the overcrowding was the fact that there was only one lavatory for so many men, most of whom were suffering from a form of dysentery; I was one of them, with severe diarrhoea, continually on the run. The boat had been adapted to alleviate the problem somewhat, in that part of the gunwale had been cut down, so that one could sit over the edge of the boat bare bottomed in full view of the Dutch women working in the field. One of my most degrading moments was when I had more or less to order off a Moroccan so that I could take advantage of this very public convenience.

We disembarked at Emmerich and were put into a train. Part of the journey was, I think, in a cattle truck, but mostly in 3rd class compartments, via Bad and Aschaffenberg to Laufen. I recall little of this journey. Some things remain with me; the growing feeling of claustrophobia as we went further and further inland leaving the sea so far behind. Then there was the immensity of the country, and as we passed through the Ruhr the great extent of its industry and also the enormous numbers of captured British and French guns and tanks and weapons. How could small Britain maintain itself against such great odds? Then again, I remember a change in the atmosphere as one entered Germany. The Dutch were a conquered nation, on the brink of unforeseeable privations as an occupied country, and yet in Holland there was colour and spirit and joy. In Germany we were in the land of the conquerors but there was no joy; all seemed as grey as the soldiers' uniforms. The towns were without colour except for some red Nazi flags, and the people purposeful but without spirit. All this naturally brought on a feeling of depression, increased by the fundamental malaise of an officer prisoner of war which I shall return to. This depression was not dispelled by the attitude of some French officers with whom I shared a carriage. Soon after they got into the train they opened their packs and disclosed large amounts of Cadburys chocolate and other foodstuffs that they had clearly taken from a British Naafi. They had foreseen what was to happen to them and had made ample preparation. We were then almost at the worst of our hunger, and I had been dreaming of chocolate; it would have been marvellous to have been able to have part of one bar of which the French had acquired so many. It sounds a small thing, but hunger magnifies the worst in us.

Laufen

So we arrived in the town of Laufen on the Austrian border on the 16th July 1940. It was about 2.a.m. and as we arched up to the prison camp, summer lightning was flickering around the mountains. The camp had been the palace of the Archbishop of Salzburg, not many miles away. It was impressive, particularly the tower over the gate through which we were herded, squat and cream coloured with a red crest over the gate itself. The buildings inside were less imposing and very crowded. The room in which I was to live, sleep, eat and read was number 66 and it had 63 or so of us in it, with three tier beds and straw palliasses to sleep on over a wooden slatted base. The choice of bed was difficult - I tried all three. The top one was far the warmest but also the stuffiest, and it was difficult to make a bed. The bottom one was fresh but bitterly cold. The middle one was warmish and only moderately stuffy, but when the man on the top got up to relieve himself, as frequently happened in those early days, he might well put his foot in the face of the man in the middle bunk as he stepped down. We had wooden tables to sit at and wooden stools to sit on.

The buildings enclosed, or nearly enclosed, two courtyards, in one of which we paraded. There were then buildings outside, a "Garage" Theatre, partly enclosing another yard, and beyond it another space called the Green Park but no longer green. Down below was the Lower Park which was sometimes out of bounds, running down towards the river Salzach, the boundary between Germany and Austria.

The main buildings were 4 storeys high, and from the top one had a wonderful view. There were the craggy looking mountains in the general direction of Berchtesgaden, and in the middle distance one could see the spires and towers of Salzburg. Running, so far as we were concerned, left handed from them ran the river Salzach, falling rapidly with plenty of white water. On the other side was the picturesque village of Oberndorf, quiet and nestling into the countryside. It was in this village that on one Christmas time the organ broke down, and the local priest wrote a poem and the organist set it to music with a view to its being sung unaccompanied that evening, as it was. This was "Stille Nacht, Heilige Nacht" - Silent Night. The beautiful views almost added to one's depression; both the mountains and the river beckoned me, and one felt all the more shut up and claustrophobic.

On our arrival we were fed reasonably well and slept. Next day we were given what was said to be the de-lousing treatment, though the doctors with us explained that we had all been in hospital and were free of lice. First of all our heads had to be run over with the cutters and then our clothes were all taken away to be baked, while we had a shower. This shower was a bit of a shock, as sharing were a number of prisoners who had been at Laufen for some weeks. Their hair was beginning to grow, but what hit one was their scraggy limbs and pot bellies, explained a bit later as we settled in. We felt that the purpose of the head shaving was not so much for health as for our degradation.

We were then admitted to the main camp and to room 66. Our first concern was to find out what had happened to our friends and relatives. We heard on the march and in the camp of some of them who had been killed - Gerald Hingley and Hutton Squire for example - but we could never hear about those who had returned safe to England. Some of my friends of course were in the camp, Derek Woodward and Tony Whitaker among others. Another unexpected one was Norman Forbes who later went to Colditz; he was in the R.A.F. and had been shot down. But there was no news of Keith or others in the 7th Worcestershire Regiment whom I knew, and of course many in my own Regiment with whom I had been so closely and recently concerned. Nor did we know what news our parents and friends in England had of us. In fact it seems that the M.O. who had treated me in the Aid Post had reported that though I was still alive there was little hope for me; I was put under a table for protection, which would not have been necessary if I was thought to be moribund. My parents had correspondence with the M.O. and were convinced of the worst. Grim as things were for me, how much worse for them! It was not until some 6 weeks later, I believe, that they heard anything of what had occurred - that was a message from the American nurse whom I had met on the march, and this they did not trust. Some days later, I think, they heard from the Red Cross that I was a prisoner of war. In the meantime there had been an obituary notice in the County Express, which I have not read; one cannot live up to an obituary. There had also been a memorial service in Broome Church; my sister-in-law Rosemary's father Richard Watson used to say I owed him two shillings which he had put into the collection at the service. The feelings of my father were shown in a reply by him to a letter of sympathy in which is included the following words,

> "Today I have had another letter from the Padre (sic) giving details of the finish. Bryan seems to have staggered into the "post" by himself and collapsed. Efforts were made to restore him but these were only partially successful though he seems to have spoken. I'll show you the letter sometime if you would care to see it, but I can't get myself to write it. "Is it well with the child?" "It is well..."

It was in September that I heard that they knew I was alive. Before this a friend of theirs who was a spiritualist wrote to my parents purporting to convey messages from me from "the other side". I met her afterwards and felt somewhat embarrassed; I felt I had let her down so badly.

We fell into the routine of life. It was similar in all the camps. There was one parade at least for us to be counted in fives, one German counting from the front and the other from behind as they went along the ranks. We were not orderly. We regarded it as a German parade which made no demands upon us. We made no attempt to be smart; we read our books or talked in a way which disgusted the Germans I have no doubt. On one occasion the German Commandant named Blatterbauer came to the parade and picked on the Earl of Hopetown to inspect. Blatterbauer was a short squat man, very pompous, and Hopetown was very tall. As Blatterbauer stood opposite him Hopetown very solemnly did a half knees bend so that they were on the same level. Not in the drill book!

There was one exception to the general shambles. On the king's official birthday the Germans were astonished to see us in our best uniform, boots clean and everything as tidy as we could make them, no books on parade and the drill as smart as could be, as on the parade ground. The next day back to normal. I suppose the Germans were told what it was all about.

Before the parade the British orderlies brought round breakfast. We were allowed, I think, one orderly, an other rank prisoner, for every 10 officers. Some ran the cookhouse and others were allotted to the various huts to keep the rooms clean and bring round the meals in big containers. Breakfast would consist of a mug of ersatz tea or coffee, and a fifth or sometimes a quarter of a loaf of rye bread, say 3 thin slices. To begin with this bread had patches of green or yellow mould on them. We were told that we could eat the green but not the yellow parts. We were not delicate feeders at the time. Later on in the day we had a bowl of thin soup and potatoes. Unfortunately these potatoes were really bad; they were marked with a dye to indicate they were not fit for human consumption, and I believe they were the cause of the pot bellies I had noticed in the shower baths and the frequent calls to the latrines by night. Later in the evening we had an issue of a small amount of margarine and sometimes a sort of paté or a small camembert cheese, or something called "Echt Kunst-honig" or "real artificial honey". Occasionally we had something called "Brotaufstreichmittel" or "something to spread on bread". This seemed to be a swede jam of some sort, highly coloured and flavoured with saccharine. Even I could not eat this. It will be noticed that no green vegetables appeared in the diet, and I used to try to improve it by picking nettles which could be found around the camp, wash them and pour the hot soup over them. This killed the sting and they were quite palatable. Our diet, we were told, provided 1450 calories a day, and did little to build us up after the wounds or diseases which had put us into hospital. I soon found, as did others, that if one climbed two flights of stairs one had a sort of momentary blackout. The Geneva Convention, with which until towards the end the Germans complied, stipulated that officers could not be compelled to work, and though we were permitted to work, to do so must have helped the German war effort. This did not apply to the other ranks, who could be compelled to work and did so in bad conditions, but often lived on farms and became friendly with the farmers. For us, apart from parades and meal times, the day was our own - and there was nothing to do. It is true there were news bulletins posted, always depressing in the extreme. I believe at the start only one or two German newspapers were admitted, and some prisoners who had lived in Nazi Germany were very good at interpreting what was written between the lines, or, more exactly, from what was left out of the papers, but we had no books or papers generally available. We got what exercise we could walking round whatever area was open to us, discussing all manner of things, food being the most insistent topic. There was also a canteen where we could in the early days buy and drink beer, and again talk. The canteen also sold such things as toothpaste and shaving requirements and a sort of soap, made up mostly of grit it seemed. Among their wares was a kind of sauce called Worcestershire Sauce, in a familiarly labelled bottle but tasting of hair lotion. Neil Perrins, who was a prisoner with us, took a very poor view of it.

There were however some other resources; there were very many talents in the camp, and many men with varied experiences who were prepared to give lectures. I remember a few of them; talks on climbing in the Himalayas, on the making of wine, on riding in the Grand National, on tea tasting, and scores of others. These talks were given more or less in public, but there were also small groups studying a number of subjects under an "expert"; a number of languages courses, and in business studies of various kinds. These were usually in small groups outside dotted about in one of the "Parks". There were also, later on, plays and concerts. Of course the female parts were played by men, which did not matter terribly in Shakespeare, but in other plays it did not always work so well. Some of the "female" actors were quite credible, and to see them shaving the next day was almost disgusting. I have one other bitter sweet memory of musical concerts. To begin with these were restricted to piano recitals, and I recall those particularly of Henry Coombe Tennant, a regular Officer and a brilliant pianist. At one stage concerts were forbidden, but the word would be passed round that he or some other would be "practising" on a certain evening, and we would all pick up our stools and proceed to the garage where this "practice" took place. I think these recitals were the most nostalgic experiences of prison life - those and the moon at which one could look and think that people at home might also be looking at it at the same time.

So we entertained ourselves as best we could from our own resources. Later we became better equipped and could greatly expand the scope of entertainment and instruction. But in spite of this, and particularly in the early years, we were faced with long periods of boredom and depression. The news, bad enough in fact but blackened by the German bulletins, and the feeling that we could take no further part in the struggle, imposed a feeling of hopelessness on us all. We did not have the surge of patriotism enjoyed by Britain, nor the fighting speeches of Churchill, to sustain us, and the best we could see in the future was an ignominious draw. Later, when the Battle of Britain was at its height, and the successes of the Germans were every day reported in the bulletins, we began to get letters from home, and to our surprise it seemed that our relatives at home had all suddenly taken to shooting, reporting large and apparently identical bags of grouse or whatever. These, we now know, were exaggerated but they cheered us immensely. But the early days were ones of depression. I found much relief in forcing myself every morning to look forward as excitedly as possible to some event during the day, even so unimportant as finding out what type of soup we were to have - there were only three; a sort of thin vegetable soup, a thin porridge and one with a piece of meat about the size of the last joint of one's thumb - or how far a bud or blossom had developed during the night.

One thing which contributed most to this feeling of depression was just hunger. We had as I have said, a loaf of bread among about five people - it varied from time to time. We took it in turns to do the cutting of the loaf into five, and the only rule thereafter was that the person doing the cutting always had the last portion, after all others had taken theirs. I found it impossible to avoid watching greedily while the cutting was taking place, and I recall realising that hunger obliterates the decent feelings that we normally have in our relationships. I can well understand people searching, almost without shame, for scraps in dustbins, and I am sure that it was hard for the kitchen staff to send out to each of the rest of us as much as they were each themselves taking. Lack of food had a degrading force, but even worse for those who smoked was the lack of cigarettes. All sorts of things were pressed into service to take tobacco's place; some smoked cherry leaves and others potato peelings. Some even picked up the fag ends left by German soldiers and made them into cigarettes. I was thankful not to have had any desire to smoke.

We stayed very much within ourselves. We each did individually with our rations what we could, and ate them on our own. We called each other by our surnames and spoke little of our own private affairs and families. It is difficult now to recall this feeling of isolation, or the reasons for it. Part of it arose perhaps from a feeling of shame at having been captured at all, though most of us would not have been able to get away even with the best of luck and courage. After some time this isolation began to break down and we got to know each other, and our feelings and fears, more clearly, and we began to call each other by our christian names. One rather coarse man in our room began to speculate on my name; knowing that I came from Worcestershire and that my first initial was B he dubbed me Bertie, as in Bertie Wooster, and Bertie I remained and remain for my fellow prisoners. I should explain that though I had been promoted to Captain just before the Battle of France began, this was only a temporary rank, and as such, as soon as I became a casualty, I, strictly speaking, reverted to my substantive rank, which was 2nd Lt. As we were put in rooms by rank I was in the company of subalterns who were my junior in age, and I did not regret this. Some of the Captains with whom I made friends would gladly have joined me in this more vigorous and joyful company.

In spite of all that I have said the life in camp gradually became a carefree one. As we began to push the problems outside a bit into the background, and to live for the day only, we began to appreciate the absence of demanding possessions. "The true pilgrim carries nothing but his lyre". In some ways too our health gradually improved; particularly those who had suffered from indigestion found that the low diet relieved it. Our exercise to start with was limited, though P.T. classes were organised; the more usual way of expanding the lungs - still important as far as I was concerned - was to walk round the perimeter wire; this was a double apron barbed wire fence ten or twelve feet high, with coiled barbed wire between the aprons. A few feet inside the wire was a trip wire - placards proclaimed that if we stepped over it we would be shot at. There were sentry boxes (goon boxes) at strategic points along the wire which was illuminated at night. For some unknown reason we always went around the wire in an anticlockwise direction, and this I believe was general throughout the camps. I noticed by the way, in Melbourne a year or so ago, that the joggers went round the park clockwise; perhaps it has something to do with the way cyclones revolve in different directions in the north and south hemispheres! We often went in pairs, discussing many subjects - food, the course of the war, any escape which was being planned, and, beyond that, impractical subjects such as philosophy and metaphysics, religion and jurisprudence, and the sort of world that would develop after the war. There were so many people from different backgrounds that this exchange of ideas was immensely stimulating.

Germans were of course frequently within the camp; they came in to take the parades, to see the Senior British officer, on searches of buildings for contraband and for other security purposes. The "ferrets" were often about with their long poles, prodding for tunnels. The German civilian orderlies also came from time to time into the camp, bringing in stores or letters and parcels, and taking out rubbish and laundry and occasionally sewage in horse or bullock-drawn tanks. There were long periods however when there were no Germans in the camp; they relied on the vigilance of the goons in the goon boxes and the sentries at the gate to prevent any escape.

One incident at Laufen I vividly remember. A young officer named Lt. Deas was standing at a window at the top of the building, sketching the landscape. A guard saw him and apparently shouted, but was either not heard or the officer did not know that the guard was shouting at him. The guard then fired at him and killed him. This had a terrible effect on us all. Quite spontaneously we took no notice of the Germans, but walked about in silence and black fury. The atmosphere was heavy with anger; the Germans clearly expected trouble, since the prisoners approaching the main staircase were suddenly confronted by guards with a machine gun at the ready. No doubt the Senior British Officer demanded an explanation from the Kommandant, and sent an urgent complaint to the Protecting Power, but the reaction of all of us to this unforgettable act must have jolted the Germans, who were probably fully ashamed of the incident anyway. It was some days before light-heartedness returned.

It was at Laufen that I first came into contact with a real escape attempt. A tunnel had been started in the store under our room. The only person whom I can remember being on it was Pat Reid who subsequently escaped from Colditz. On the night of the break they spent the first part of the night in our room, though we saw little of them. I do not remember now how far they got before being recaptured. As always, the escape lit up the camp and the morale was lifted, but more of this later. The story of this escape is well told in Pat Reid's "The Colditz Story".

As the summer faded we began to get letters and parcels from home, and from other countries. The only individual parcels which could be sent from home were clothes parcels, one a quarter, and as winter approached these were extremely valuable. Other parcels arrived through the kindness of those in neutral states, and of those in countries that had been overrun. I had parcels of sardines from my father's old school friend named Tait in Portugal, and also, through Rotary, of food from America. Then there were small food parcels, no doubt saved from their own rations, from Lies Goedkoop and Fru Benthin of Holland and Denmark. One can never repay this sort of kindness, and the addition of even small amounts of food made a great difference to one's energy and stamina. The main supplement to our rations, however, was the Red Cross parcel. We seldom had a whole parcel each per week as was intended, and to begin with it was probably more like one among four. A whole parcel would consist of a tin of meat (spam, or meat and veg), biscuits, milk (evaporated or powdered), butter or margarine, dried fruit, a tinned pudding, packeted cheese, tea and a quarter pound bar of chocolate. This was a typical parcel, but there were variations from time to time. I have said that on the German rations exercise such as climbing two flights of stairs brought on a form of exhaustion. On half a Red Cross parcel a week I could play two games of basket ball or similar game a week before this exhaustion set in; on a whole parcel I could take any amount of exercise and be unaffected - so critical was our diet at the time.

I have some notes of our Christmas of 1940. It seemed difficult to look forward to it in such circumstances. The notes however say,

> "But now the day itself has arrived. I for one have been surprised at the suppressed excitement we have felt from the beginning of the day. Awake by about 6.45 (4.45 G.M.T) I got up and had English tea - a tremendous impetus to the excitement - washed and went to Communion at 7.45. The Recreation Room was packed, people standing at the back, and this made it an impressive service. There was also a Scottish service in the Theatre and another C of E in the Recreation Room at 8.30. After Communion I returned to Room 66, wishing everyone Merry Christmas en route, and ate my breakfast consisting of a bit of bread and Red Cross syrup. Then parade, everyone in good form and no "room count".

> And so back to the Recreation Room to morning service, an animated service and a good sermon by the Padre of the Seaforths. I had had an invitation to drink wine with Derek Woodward, so I retired to Room 80, having got my bottle of Mauhaust,(as far as I remember a rather sour Riesling bought at an exorbitant price in the Canteen), and arranged my place for lunch. Room 80 party consisted of Derek Woodward the Ram and Tony Whitaker, and we had a very pleasant party. Lunch was terrific. The cookhouse had saved a week's issue of meat, I am told, so we had a decent stew and mashed potatoes and stewed fruit and the wine we had bought. Sleep took up most of the afternoon, and a walk".

The note goes on to say that I spent time in the afternoon going round paying calls and giving Christmas presents of cigarettes to my friends. The evening was less pleasant, as a number of my companions drank too much and were sick, which rather spoilt the day. I do not remember this happening again. One thing I noted as memorable is "the tact of the German Officer who in doing his rounds turned a blind eye to many things."

I have mentioned the Canteen on a number of occasions. Here one could buy the general requirements of living, mostly toiletries of one sort or another. To begin with we could also buy drinks of various kinds, but I think this died out as the war went on. Where, you may ask, did the money come from with which we could make the purchases? It was rather a complicated financial transaction. We had, during our imprisonment, a credit building up from our British Army pay. The Germans, in the meantime, opened accounts in our camps for each of us, and credited us with the pay of an equivalent rank in the German Army, which was less than the British pay, and would be met at the end of the war by a transfer from our accounts in Britain. We could withdraw money from our German accounts, not in ordinary marks but in lagermarks, bits of paper like monopoly money. With this we could buy goods in the Canteen. Alongside this there grew up a sophisticated system within the camp of Exchange and Mart, run by entrepreneurial prisoners. Certain goods, items from food parcels or clothing etc., were from time to time in oversupply, and they could be exchanged, at a varying exchange rate, for other items in demand. There was a unit of currency based, generally, on the cigarette. We had a small issue of German cigarettes from time to time and later on a number of English cigarettes too.

My notes are resumed on 18th February 1941 and on the next day it is recorded that a tunnel had been discovered in the Recreation Room. Three days later I noted that I had volunteered to go to Titmoning, a smaller camp. "Anything for a change". After more rumours of a move it appeared on 25th February that the occupants of Room 66, with others, were to move to Posen, but it was not until the 4th March that we left, starting at 5.30 a.m. and marching to the station. I noted "Glad to finish with Laufen". There must have been mixed feelings, as we went through the gates to the cheers of many friends from whom we were sad to part. But the spirit of the camp was bad. The younger people felt that the older "dug out majors" had got themselves into positions of authority, and were not above running a racket or two for their own benefit. If anyone was to have rations greater than others it should have been the young - some were only about 19 - and not those who claimed preference because they had the responsibilities for running some department of the camp life. Perhaps the criticisms were ungrounded, but it was a relief to leave this large camp with the prospect of a smaller and more unified camp before us. Besides this, as on any move, we were assured by the Germans that we were going to a camp with much better conditions.

Poland

We went by train with wooden seats to Regensburg and through the night to Leipzig and Cottbus. On the 7th March we arrived at Posen,

> "a horrid city. We are escorted by Uhlans and carry our kit 2 miles. We are marched across a drawbridge into a cavern. Frightful accommodation, but I am with Peter Conder and V. Hollom so it might be worse. Three parades a day. Walk in the available part of the ditch. It is frightful, but the worse it is the more we laugh".

Posen was in fact a very smoky town in a very flat and featureless countryside, badly bombed but with friendly Poles in evidence. We approached the camp over a moat - and beyond that was the entrance, forbidding and badly lit, as though leading to some derelict underground station. We were then told that far from this being a better camp it was a reprisal camp for alleged ill treatment of German prisoners in Canada. It seemed that they had been put into a fort there, but Canadians who knew it described it as being very commodious and comfortable. Our "fort" was not that. It had been built centuries before, to face the Russians. It was surrounded by a ditch (the moat) onto which the rooms, in two storeys, looked out, and it was covered by an earth roof. I was fortunate in being on the top storey, and from one window - but not of course from the ground floor windows - we could with difficulty just see the sky and the bottoms of the trees on the other side of the ditch. We were 27 in the room, in two-tier beds. There was one table, and we were lucky to have 10 stools; I see from my notes,

> "Plenty of washing bowls are given us, and one eating bowl between two officers: no other tools".

We had fleas in large quantities, and used to put up a tally of "kills" every night, 184 being recorded one day. Lice were worse, and harder to eradicate. There were mice and rats, and a fear that there might be typhus-carrying black rats.

> "Our latrine arrangements for about 600 consist at the moment of one urinal for which we have to queue, and 8 seats, both of unbelievable odour".

The seats were of an interesting construction, built round a centre drainpipe, octagonal therefore in shape. There were four hand operated water pumps, one in complete darkness, for washing ourselves, our utensils and clothes, and to draw water which had to be boiled for drinking.

Our exercise was taken in walking the dank and dark vaulted passages, or in the "available part of the ditch". The ditch was very wet and muddy, receiving the droppings from both walls. Down the middle was a gutter full of stagnant water. Outside the latrines ran the foul water drains, one of which had apparently burst and run into the gutter.

> "The air is not fresh. The ditch is about 300 yards in length, and 20 yards across, so there is quite a good straight slither, if you can make it".

We were shut into our rooms at 2100 hours and expected to find relief in a bucket.

Gradually things improved. The food was not too bad, and parades were reduced from 3 to 2 per day. We were issued with spoons and sheets. A canteen was opened, and we were no longer confined to our rooms at night. Best of all we were occasionally allowed out on parole walks. The other conditions remained the same, however, and we were glad therefore to be told at the end of March that we were to be moved to a new camp the following week. General Fortune, who had commanded the Highland Division captured at St.Valery and was the Senior British Officer at this camp, may have helped to engineer the move. There was a high-powered visit from the Swiss Red Cross and in the course of the inspection a board with a louse tally on it was shown to him. The German Officer in attendance soundly denied that there were any lice, upon which General Fortune called up an officer who had been specially prepared and was alive with the beastly things. He should have been mentioned in despatches for outstanding devotion to duty! Anyway on the 3rd April we left without regret and marched to Posen station.

We arrived late at night at Thorn and entered another fort on the same lines as the one at Posen but bigger and lighter. Many from Laufen were already there, Norman Forbes among them. The room was light and airy, we sat down at tables with necessary implements - quite good conditions and only 20 in a room. My note says,

> "There are, thank heaven, hot baths (showers} and a delousing room. The ablutions are not good, consisting of about four benches of ten dribbles each, but this is, I suppose, better than the Posen pump. Among the advantages are a chapel

and a trumpeter who does bugle calls (the Lambeth Walk}. The roof on which we are allowed to go is leafy and abounds in birds, in particular nightingales sing to us all day. The sports Platz is about 20 minutes walk away and the trees are in bloom and life very fresh".

We were there until June and the whole of the Poland episode gave us a new view of the world and the war.

As we had passed through Europe on the train for Poland we had seen German troops and material going down south towards Greece and Yugoslavia to aid the Italians struggling there. Now in Poland, looking East across to the Vistula and beyond, we saw from the flow of armaments going East the preparations Germany was making for war on the Eastern front. Russia was in theory bound to Germany by a pact, but for once the rumours, coming from the Poles, were true, that Germany and Russia were preparing for war. That must have been one of the best opportunities for escape that existed during the whole of the years of imprisonment, since the Poles were of course strongly anti-German, and would give all the support they could. In fact Norman Forbes and Airey Neave did get out of the camp, dressed, improbably, as French prisoners, and they were near to the Russian border when they were recaptured. They thus became qualified for Colditz, from which Airey Neave subsequently escaped and got back home.

Biberach and Warburg

It was becoming more and more clear that we were on one of the main supply routes to a likely attack on Russia, and in June 1941 we were moved almost the breadth of Germany to Biberach south of

Ulm. This was, I think, the best camp I was in, partly because there were not too many of us and it was clean, and partly because the spirit of the place was so good. We were in well built barrack blocks in gritted parade grounds, with excellent bathing facilities. A typical day is noted as,

> "up at 7.30, Breakfast 8. Parade 8.30, Work French Spanish German Law 9-12, 12 lunch, 12-4 Books etc., 4 tea, 6 Deck Tennis, 7.30 supper. Thereafter visiting and reading of various sorts".

As I was busy on a tunnel at the time the word "work" was somewhat disguised. Of that escape attempt and others I will say something later. What with the good morale and the comparative freedom within the camp, and the special exhilaration wh1¢h the work on the tunnel generated, this was I think a time upon which I look back with a pleasure which I did not feel elsewhere.

Our camp received a large intake of those captured in Greece and Crete. I had been told that Tony Southall, later of the firm of Solicitors Manby and Steward of Wolverhampton, had come into the camp. I had gone over to the new blocks to try to find him, and had seen the name G.O. Evers Swindell on a door. He was a New Zealander, my second cousin once removed. I was able to help him with clothes etc., and later became Godfather to his son.

We were only about 50 miles from the Swiss border; the mountains of Austria and Switzerland reared up in the distance, and attempts at escape came fast and furiously. I had been recaptured after my escape attempt and had not been long back in the camp, after being able to do only 3 days of my punishment of 10 days solitary confinement when we were moved in October 1941 to a camp at Warburg near the town of Kassel towards the north of the country. For some unknown reason none of the 23 who escaped through the tunnel and were recaptured were sent to Colditz, so we all journeyed together.

Warburg was a very large camp; part of it was brick built barrack blocks, and part wooden houses raised on brick pillars. I was in one of the wooden houses. The winter of 1941/42 was bitterly cold, but by that time our stock of warm clothes had built up a bit, and we survived. It was sad however to see how others were faring. There was near our camp a large camp of Russian prisoners who were working under the Germans. One could see them being marched past the wire, thin and listless and badly clothed against the cold. By some means - I do not know what - we managed to divert some of our food which was, with Red Cross Parcels, fairly plentiful at the time, to the Russians' kitchen, and this small amount of extra food seemed almost to put a spring in their step. I well remember one dark night when the R.A.F. made their first 1000 ton raid on the Ruhr. We could hear the distant explosions, long protracted, of the bombs, and when this was over the Russian camp burst into full throated song, eerie and haunting, a powerful expression, we thought, of exhilaration and thanks.

Here again we turned our minds to escaping. As I shall deal with this in another section I will only mention two episodes about this here. One of my friends, Peter Conder, was a great ornithologist and would sit for hours on his stool with a note book, putting down in minute detail the doings of birds both inside and outside the camp. On one occasion he was taken by the German guards and questioned about his clearly significant activity. He managed after a time to establish his innocence, and was allowed to continue his observations undisturbed. On some occasions this proved very useful, as he was able to act as a "stooge" without causing any suspicion. The word "significant", by the way, was in common use about someone who was on some sort of escape activity and was trying hard to look as if he wasn't.

Another is the story of an escape manqué. Fairly close to the wire was a barrack block inside the wire housing prisoners. Outside the wire, not too far off, was another brick block inhabited by Germans. Some would-be escapers discovered that one end of the block was used as a store room, an excellent place into which to come up at the end of a tunnel. All went well with a tunnel or "groove" as it was often called, until the tunnellers suddenly found that they had broken through into the German Officers Mess wine cellar. This rather changed their plans, and after a time there were empty bottles around. This must clearly be remedied, and the bottles were refilled with the only liquid the would-be escapers had readily available, and recorked. At this point your imagination must take over and tell what tale it wishes.

This camp was eventful in all sorts of ways. One feature for me was the 7 days I spent in the cooler finishing my 10 days solitary confinement after the escape attempt at Biberach. When one lives in very close proximity to a large number of men, a few days in solitary is no unpleasant thing, particularly when one is allowed to take in books, as I was. I read a lot of Shakespeare, and also "Their England", whose account of a cricket match is one of the most amusing passages I know. Outside, the rest of the camp were suffering one of those alarms and excursions to which the camp seemed particularly prone, namely one of the most savage searches my fellow prisoners ever experienced. Things were thrown out of the window and generally treated without any respect at all. This all passed me by, though when I returned I found that my best jacket had had ink spilt over it. My laughter and their fury made a very striking contrast.

A very sad event was the death of a young Scotsman in a tunnelling accident. This tunnel had electric light at the face, carried from the mains by electric wires. Somehow or another, while working on the face, he was electrocuted, and could not be got out. The tunnel had already extended beyond the wire, so the position had to be disclosed to the Germans, who dug his body out. Though I did not know him well his popularity with those who did increased the feeling of grief throughout the camp.

This was a camp in which many of us turned our minds to wine making. I remember producing a concoction in an old bucket; the brew was made from currants and raisins hoarded from many Red Cross Parcels, and we swore it tasted splendid, though it must have been terribly young, a sort of Warburg Nouveau. I do not remember hearing of any spirits being distilled in this or indeed other camps, but it may well have happened.

We had been there about a year, and had spent in all an unthinkable 2½ years as prisoners, when rumours were rife about another move. It was I think, in October 1942 that we finally moved. We went, as usual, by train, and I should mention a feature of all our train journeys. We were always on the look-out for opportunities to jump the train - a hazardous enterprise - and there were often one or two fewer prisoners on Appel at the end of the journey. These journeys were usually of some duration, and I formed the habit of sleeping on the luggage rack. A sudden jolt might throw one out, I suppose, but fortunately I slept reasonably undisturbed. One or two then slept on the floor and others on the wooden benches, all more or less at full stretch. I think my bed was probably the most comfortable. During the day it was interesting to see the countryside and the dull shut-in look of the people as they went about their affairs. Our food was generally hunks of bread and German sausage, quite appetizing and a change from our normal camp fare.

Eichstätt

The camp at which we arrived in due course was at Eichstätt in the middle of Germany. It is an interesting town. Strongly catholic, it was a prince bishopric founded in 741 by St. Willibald and the fine cathedral held the bones of St. Walpurga, a British born saint. The town had been very pro-English in the Middle Ages apparently, right up to this century in fact. It was a pretty little town, set on the river Altmuhl. The power in the land was the Convent, whose Abbess was, as will be seen, a strong personality and strongly anti-Nazi.

The camp itself to which we marched lay in a really lovely valley, on a slight slope some little distance from the river, along which ran a railway line, and a corresponding slope covered with trees opposite us. It was beautifully quiet and peaceful; the camp was, the Germans told us, escape proof.

On entering any camp the first thing we had to do was to go through a search and be registered. Sometimes it was pretty intensive and of course there was plenty of contraband to be got through. On one or two occasions I was deputed to get through the search a map of Germany, drawn on silk and very detailed. This I used to fold into the handle of my shaving brush. The handle was of wood, and I could unscrew it from the brush part, and I had gouged out a hole big enough to take the map. I used to dry out the brush so that I could unscrew the handle, insert the map and rescrew it; if I then dampened it I could not unscrew it, nor could the Germans. Dry it again after the search and I could retrieve the map. I also had another ploy. I had seen in the paper a notice of the death in battle of someone named Evers, a Ritter Kreutztrager, a high military honour. I cut it out and put it in my pocket. The first question a searcher put was "What is your name?" I told him and he would say, "How do you spell it?" and I would produce the obituary notice and show it and say, "I spell it like this". The sight of the name and decoration produced quite an effect, and prompted the question, "Is he a relative of yours?" to which I was a bit evasive. The search of my things was then perfunctory.

So we entered the camp proper. It was empty on our arrival and it merits some description. Inside the camp ran a very presentable road, the Lagerstrasse, running from one end of the camp to the gate, rarely used, at the far end. Fronting this road were buildings of brick, on the left, to start with, two-storey living quarters, Blocks I II and III backing on to the wire; on the right of the road opposite Block III was an administration block, with library, canteen, cookhouse etc. Further on, back on the left, and close to the far gate, was the hospital block, dentists surgery and so on. All this was on the top of a bank falling away on the right, and below it a large area running the length of the camp, first at the end nearest the main gate providing a sizeable sports ground on which we played cricket and other games; there was also a rink for skating in the winter, doubling during the summer as a five-a-side hockey pitch. Beyond that was a kitchen garden in which we could grow vegetables to supplement the rations; beyond that again, a large number of wooden huts known as the "Garden City", housing most of the camp's inhabitants. Having set the scene I can return to our entrance into our home - though of course we did not know it - for two and a half years. There was an interesting prelude to it.

We were paraded on the main sports ground which acted also as a parade ground. We were addressed by a tall dark officer who turned out later to be very dull and stupid. What he said was this: "British Officers, I am your new interpreter and I must tell you I have been in England and have learned the English way of life, and I have learnt the English sense of humour". The idea of solemnly learning a sense of humour seemed to us to be exceedingly comical and we burst into roars of laughter. The interpreter was furious, and obviously feared a riot or something, as the guards on the bank above us trained their machine guns on us in a menacing way. Our laughter had to go underground.

The camp had been inhabited by Belgian prisoners who had not been too tidy in their ways. One of their habits which endeared them to us however, was their tendency to hoard. All sorts of useful things could be found by an enthusiastic seeker, and stocks of food were found and appropriated. Perhaps they were moved in a hurry. Anyway we wished them well! It was a potentially clean camp with plenty of recreation ground, cooking facilities and above all a library. This was stocked by books provided mainly I think, by the Y.M.C.A. Throughout our stay it grew in size and the variety of its subjects. There was also a theatre or concert hall in the centre administration block.

I have mentioned cooking facilities. There was a good central cookhouse which not only provided us with a hot soup at midday but also could take our private pies, cakes and so on, as I remember on a rota basis, for supper. There was however a curious tendency of prisoners of war to create their own cooking apparatus in their rooms. The most obvious one was an oven. The rooms were all heated by a continental stove, and against it we erected a brick oven plastered with clay. Where the mud and the bricks came from I do not remember, but I cannot think it was all illicit. The Germans were trying hard to make it a reasonably comfortable camp - the war by then was clearly not going to be a walk-over for them - and bricks and some clay and possibly cement may have been provided. The increased comfort and the usual statement that the camp was escape-proof would, it was hoped, persuade us to settle down to peaceful pursuits until the war ended. We fell into a routine fairly quickly - for much of the time mine was as follows:-

6.30	Up and over to the library to read there until breakfast and parade and to book a place for the morning.
8.00	Breakfast, (Issue of 115th loaf bread and ersatz coffee) and parade.
C. 9.00	Reading in the library, where it was quiet and one could make notes.
c. 12.30	Lunch. (Issue of soup) Afternoon, reading in the sun, taking some exercise and walking and writing.
C. 5.00	Tea, (Issue of ersatz tea and later real tea) and parade.
C. 6.00	Preparing evening meal from Red Cross parcels. Evening, reading and writing, and listening to music on gramophone.
9.30	Listening to B.B.C news in skeleton form - when the secret radio was working.
10.30	Bed.

I am often, naturally, asked whether we knew at all how the war was going. My reply is that we knew, in fact, rather more than the people at home. We had the German papers with their occasional admissions which they tried to explain away. Then there were new prisoners being brought into the camp with information about action on the battlefield or in the air; there were German guards who could tell of conditions on the eastern front and in bombed cities, and, after the first year or so of war, we had the nine o'clock news almost every night. This was received on a secret radio. It was interesting that when the Hood and the Bismark were both sunk this was reported on both British and German news bulletins, but the German guards said that they did not think the German news was true that the Hood was sunk, but that this was only referred to as an excuse or compensation for the loss of the Bismark. Propaganda, long continued, loses its edge.

There were of course interruptions to this quiet life. There were concerts of reasonable standard and plays above average, as we had one or two good professional actors among us. I recall one performance of "French Without Tears" and an excellent Hamlet with Michael Goodliffe as Hamlet. He appeared later quite a lot on the stage and T.V. - I saw him in London in a Chekov play. Michael Langham, later - more or less - put the Shakespeare Theatre at Stratford Ontario on the map, and was acting as a consultant, and directing within the theatre complex, when I was in Stratford Ontario in 1983. Desmond Llewellyn has appeared, at any rate until quite recently, on television.

We were also allowed from time to time to go to the town to the cinema or theatre on parole. I remember seeing Baron Munchausen in colour - the first cinema film in colour that I had seen. We also went to the circus. The young acrobats and performers were no doubt called up, and we had before us those who were over military age, but I am sure that none of them, particularly the women whose beauty had waned as their weight had waxed, ever had a more rapturous welcome and acclaim than they received from us, starved as we were of such excitements.

Other interruptions were less happy. One day in about April 1943 a sudden Appel was called, and 100 Canadians were put into handcuffs and taken out of the camp. This, we were told, was a reprisal for the order made by the Canadians on their attack on Dieppe to handcuff their prisoners as they got them back to England. A few days later another Appel was suddenly called. With some friends I was, as I remember, celebrating someone's birthday in the Canteen. Adopting Drake's principle we waited to go down to the parade ground until we had finished our drinks so when we fell in we were well on the left of the line. We were all informed that Churchill, after the handcuffing of the Canadians, had put into handcuffs a hundred German prisoners so Hitler had said he would handcuff three times any number that Churchill handcuffed. This he could easily do; I was one of the 300, being one of the latest on parade.

These handcuffs were messy little things which kept one's hands close together so that one's wrists almost touched and one could do very little with them. We were placed all together, with the Canadians who were brought back to the camp, in the brick buildings at the end of the Lagerstrasse nearest the main gate. How we should have fared for long I do not know, but someone soon found a key to fit the cuffs and within an hour we were all free. We had occasional visits from guards and had to put the handcuffs on again, which was a bore - a cry of "Goon Up" alerted us to a visitation, and indeed later on the guards themselves, who disapproved of the whole exercise, called "Goon Up" as they came into the block. After a time it all became much more civilised. The handcuffs themselves were replaced by a set with two cuffs connected with a longish chain,

59

giving much more range of movement. Quite apart from this they could be opened by such a piece of metal as a scissors blade. Towards the end of the period of handcuffing the German guards used to bring the cuffs in before parade and leave them on a stool. We would then put them on for any parade, and keep them at all other times under our mattress, returning them to the stool for the guard to collect in the evening: satisfaction for everyone. Without this, the period of shackling, about 13 months I think, would have been very wearing.

I have referred to the parole visits to the town and the circus and cinema there. During the 2½ years we were at the camp in Eichstätt we were given other concessions on parole. We were allowed out on walks in the beautiful countryside, providing a very welcome - though infrequent - reminder of liberty. There was a problem here however. Our parole prevented us from doing anything to aid an escape, and it would be impossible for a would-be escaper to go for a walk without spying out the land. Some of us refrained from going on walks on that account if we were planning an escape, or indeed helping in one where it might be thought we intended to escape.

There was another activity which, towards the end of the war, we were allowed - again on parole. This was to supplement our fuel stocks which would otherwise have been running low, by going into the countryside and digging up old tree stumps and bringing them back into the camp where they would be sawn up into logs. There were two brothers in our mess at one time, who were the organisers of the "stump party" and were permanently on it; other volunteers were added a bit later on. One of them told us of the hard work they were doing and how hungry it made them. Full of sympathy we gave them rather more than their share of the rations - until we found out from the additional volunteers that the work was not particularly arduous, and the stumpers were getting far better rations than we were in the camp and were really very well fed. I went on two or three of the stumping expeditions myself, and the manual exercise there, and the sawing work in the camp which followed, improved considerably our health and strength.

So the long 2½ years spent in Eichstätt went by, years of intrinsic boredom sustained only by the interests we made for ourselves, years also increasingly difficult, it now seems to me, by relationships fraying for trivial reasons. I had, fortunately, in addition to the distractions I have mentioned already, and escape attempts which from time to time lit up our existence, two sustained activities which made my life in captivity a little less useless. I do not remember exactly how it arose, but I was asked to do some sustained coaching for the Bar exams. There were three people involved - Robin Pritchard, Henry Cleaver and Phil Dennison. I was to take them in Land Law, Conveyancing, Equity and Trusts and Probate and Divorce. Other people, barristers I think, were to deal with other subjects. The course was a three year one I believe, but I was only involved in the 2½ years we were at Eichstätt. The books were obtained through the Y.M.C.A. and we worked fairly intensively; I had of course to prepare the topic for the next day's session, but it was all very informal and we formed happy relationships. The "students" were enabled, very much towards the end of our stay in Eichstätt, to take the Bar exams which barristers in the camp invigilated. There were, I was told afterwards, five people who got "Honours" in the exams, and our three were among them, and Henry Cleaver got a prize of £70. It was no doubt worth something to them to have the practical experience, that I already had, at their disposal, but for me it was I feel more valuable, as I was able to keep my legal knowledge of these subjects fresh and up to date. I also used to go through problems with one or two others, among them John Peyton and Freddie Corfield, who subsequently became Leader of the House of Commons and Secretary of Aircraft Production respectively.

Another pursuit was even more relaxing. Peter Conder whom I have already mentioned as a bird watcher, found that a goldfinch, Carduelis Carduelis Carduelis, was building in a tree very close to our block. He conceived the idea of watching it every moment of the day, noting its movements and its calls and recording the timing of its visits to the nest and its absence, and its song as it did its various trips to and from the nest. Eventually, on his return home, Peter brought out a monograph on the subject. He required help, and this I, and others, gave him to some extent, and I often used to watch and take notes when he was off duty; it was a very exhaustive affair. As I was on an escape project at the time and the tension was inclined to build up, this was a very useful pastime, which demanded concentration on so beautiful an object as a goldfinch.

I should perhaps tell of an event in which I provided light relief for a time to the whole camp. I have mentioned that in addition to Red Cross Parcels we occasionally received parcels from other sources. One source which provided me with food parcels for a short time before America came into the war was Rotary International, organised in some way by my father who was a Rotarian and very helpful these parcels were. I had had two I think, when I was handed a slip to fetch another. This was in the days when one went with a tray filled with bowls and jars and containers of all sorts, since the guards would open everything and tip it out into whatever was available, and if there were not enough containers the jam might be tipped onto the pilchards. So burdened I duly turned up at the parcels hatch; the parcel was found and opened, and a packet of tea was extracted, slit and handed over. Next, to my confusion and disappointment, came a pair of knickers, followed by other items of female underclothing, held up by the guard to the amusement and admiration of all. It was the joke of the camp, and I was not allowed to keep them, though it would have been hard to go through the gates to freedom disguised only in these scanty and diaphanous garments.

Escaping Biberach

The one subject which we only talked about with great reserve was escaping. We might know that a tunnel was being dug somewhere in one area or other of the camp but we did not enquire into it, though one usually had an idea when the day of the breaking of the tunnel or the attempt to go through the gate was likely to take place, and the tension in the camp began to build up. It is now time to discuss some of the escapes with which I was concerned or knew about.

In a foolish moment I wrote home, informing my father, by a clumsy code we had established between us, that I had got out of the camp by a tunnel. I had a very frosty reaction; never must I try this again. That was a natural attitude for people at home. They must have thought that as I had surprisingly escaped death I must now, as a girlfriend wrote to me, leave it to them to finish the war. We were out to grass and must wait patiently and gratefully for the end.

Why then did we try to escape? One reason was that we were still soldiers and it is the duty of officers to escape. There was a story which was told of an officer in the camp named O'Sullivan. After his capture in France his father, who was himself an army officer, wrote to him with the words "O'Sullivans are not captured". Later the father was himself captured in some other theatre of war. Meanwhile O'Sullivan junior escaped from

Germany and wrote to his father "O'Sullivans escape". I cannot report on any sequel - I have told this to show that we all felt some guilt in the fact that we were captured, and new prisoners were glad to find any listener to their story of how they were taken, rationalising it to show how impossible it was for them to get away. If you had heard the cries of talkers in the night in the early days you would have been struck by the agony of mind which sleep unlocked. The circumstances of my own capture made this rationalisation fairly simple. I was most concerned for young R.A.F. Officers who were dining in the mess one night and a day or so later were being dumped in penny numbers into prison camp. Army officers had at least been away from home for some time and living rough while the battle proceeded.

There was, moreover another need, quite as fundamental. We were trying to escape from something more devitalising than our crowded and unnatural conditions and the essential loneliness and boredom of those early days. During the phoney war and the Battle of France, our purposes could not have been more clear cut. These were to stand in the way of the enemy's advance, to look after our men and materials, and then to comply with the instincts of self preservation. On our capture all these purposes which formed the basis of our lives were cut away; our ability to stop the advance of Germany had gone, we had no men or materials, or anything else, for which we were responsible, and as for self preservation our future depended on the will of another; we were "as dead things that the waves push". It was this vacuum of purpose that was I think what we were most trying to escape from. If some of us got away and back home we had all of us, in a subtle and very limited way, inflicted a defeat on our captors, and the very endeavour built a comradeship that only work together for a common and worthy objective, spiced with a little danger, can provide. The mere fact of getting out of the camp, of having broken through the defences of our immediate captors, had a remarkable effect on our morale.

   The first escape attempt with which I was concerned was at Biberach, in sight of the Swiss Alps, soon after our arrival from Poland in June 1941. I became involved in an odd way. One of our Battery Commanders, a regular major who had been posted to us shortly before embarkation, had apparently packed up during the Battle of France, and was replaced by another regular major named Bill Mercer, whom I first met in prison camp. He was the sort of man who always managed to get in on anything good - he had a nose for anything which was a bit under cover. He had somehow become involved in one of the two tunnels being driven from the camp, and after it had been started he asked me to join him. One of these tunnels was from the latrine or Abort near the wire. I must explain that the latrines in this camp were glorified earth closets. There was a very large trench and over it a row of perhaps eight seats all linked together and with no divisions between them. They were emptied periodically. Some keen escaper had decided to start a tunnel under one of the end seats by driving into the wall of the trench. I am glad to say that the tunnel I was to help on was the other one. This ran from a room in a block near the wire and had its entry by a square cut in the floor immediately under a stove. This stove which stood on a slab could be moved to one side; the square hole had been cut in the composition floor under the slab and a wooden trap had been made to fit it. After our working hours this could be put in position, covered with dust from the composition floor and the slab and the stove replaced upon it.

   When one went to work on the face one would get undressed and put on a pair of "Long Johns" or something like that, kept for the purpose in the chamber under the trap. One would then lower oneself through the hole into the chamber, and fold oneself in the very confined space so that one could crawl down, headfirst, fairly steeply to get under the foundations of the block. The tunnel then ran level for a short way to beyond the wire and then began to rise fairly steeply, as the field at which we were aiming sloped down to the wire. I must explain that there was always the difficulty of getting rid of the soil in a tunnel, and since at Biberach the whole area was covered with a form of tarmac the only place for the soil to go was in the roof, which incidentally collapsed under the weight soon after we all left the camp. This difficulty with the soil meant that the size of the tunnel had to be restricted; it was in fact 1ft. 6ins. high and 1ft. 10ins. wide, not high enough to move along on hands and knees, only on elbows and toes. As the tunnel grew in length this became quite testing, and though it was very good for the stomach muscles it was very bad for the elbows, and we got bursitis or what we called "excavator's elbow". Another problem was the air supply; we soon had to devise a pump to force air to the face but the chief difficulty was the provision of pipes to carry this fresh air, and the best we could do was with rolls of paper. The lighting to begin with was by means of "fat lamps" made with fat ration that we had from time to time as an alternative to butter or margarine. It was better burnt than eaten. We soon had to introduce a form of electric lighting. The tunnel was revetted with bed boards, generously provided by all and sundry to the detriment of their sleep. About halfway under the wire was a passing place just two men wide; in this lay the second man on the shift, in my recollection after he had worked on the face for his half hour or so there. It was his duty, when the man at the face had filled a small metal box on runners with soil and had given two tugs on the string, to pull the box back and then send it to the chamber under the floor to get it stored there temporarily. An empty box would then be pulled up by the face worker for further filling.

At the face one would hack away with a knife and
a bit of angle iron procured from somewhere. After a while one got good at it, but there were times when one met a rock or something impeding one's progress and then, lying in this confined space, one's only purpose in life was to get that stone out. There was nothing else which competed in any way with this one overriding objective. As we went on, the air got worse and worse and we could only work up front for a maximum of 20 minutes, gasping all the time. When we came back to the chamber under the floor we lay panting and revelling in the fresh air there. If one put a candle down into this chamber however, the flame went out at once, so one cannot understand how one could have worked in the foul air at the face. It was of course even worse when there was an alert and the trap and stove had temporarily to be placed over the hole. Fortunately there was no mining inspector.

Bit by bit we extended the tunnel, rising all the time, to about 45 yards, and the day for the "break" approached. The "Abort" tunnel had been discontinued and many of the workers on it were tagged on to our party, so that in the end there were 26 to go out, and lots were cast for positions. This was in some ways unfortunate, since Bill Mercer was placed high up on the list, and I was 25, so it was likely we should not meet, and we should each go on our own. When the day arrived, on 13th September 1941, we started to collect in the room with our belongings, but the whole camp knew what was up. I recall extraordinary scenes on the "campus", a great feeling of excitement with people sending messages to their people at home, wishing each other well and saying goodbye and shaking hands. It rather resembled a scene on a main line railway station, and what the sentries made of it I do not know - very little apparently.

My recollections of the moments before we got out of the tunnel are vague. I remember suddenly realising that there was someone behind me and I could not move either way and for the first time I was attacked by almost unbearable claustrophobia. I think this was before the opening was made and fresh air percolated down the tunnel. It took a long time to complete the excavation, and we had, after emerging from the hole, to crawl for about three quarters of an hour over a field of stubble under the eyes of the guards in the goonboxes before reaching cover. The fact that 26 of us managed to achieve this shows some lack of zeal and watchfulness on the part of the guards. If any of us had sneezed the searchlights would have been turned on us and anything could have happened. Bill Mercer had of course disappeared, but fortunately I joined up with David Stebbings, a young friend from the Oxfordshire and Buckinghamshire Light Infantry, and we set off together in the grey light of the growing day.

In fact, so late were we that as we went up a country road we were met by someone probably going to Mass, as it was a Sunday morning. What this person thought of us in our battledress, no doubt filthy from the soil of the tunnel, I do not know. We realised that we must get to ground as quickly as we could and we found a thicket with just about adequate cover; as we went in we thought we were being observed and hid ourselves as best we could. This was fortunate, as later on that day a man came and peered into the small copse, and was obviously looking for someone; fortunately he went away eventually without finding us. It was a near thing. So the day went by and night at last fell. It was interesting to see how alert the sentries now were, with the searchlights continually lighting up the field of stubble over which we had crawled the previous night. The exhilaration of being outside the wire was of course immense, but we had a terribly strong feeling of exposure and solitude. We could not safely think of the warmth of the camp and of an evening cup of cocoa with our friends.

Vincent Hollom left a description of the happenings in the camp on the day of our departure in a letter for me if I was re-captured and whisked off to another camp, as might well have happened. It read as follows:-

> "It enters my head Bertie, to put you down
> a note about today's activities. We heard early that all of you had got out and took steps to make a prodigious breakfast and to take books and warm clothes onto parade. We need not have bothered, for Gemmell behaved in his usual delightful way - and never a sign of pique. On reaching our Company and receiving Brush's Report he observed: 'Ein in Revier; und sieben spazieren. Gut!' and affected great surprise when eventually he found a Company in full strength. He told Tod another parade "with all the theatricals" might be necessary later but for himself dismissed us with pleasure.
>
> This was commonly agreed to be uncommonly sporting, an opinion fortified when Gemmell returned alone for a glance round Block 6. After a quick look at the room the opening and the pictures he withdrew - pausing to congratulate Tod on his way.
>
> Of course, they easily found the outlet and produced a sentry for it and packs of dogs, which put on a

brave show for the assembled mob. And all the German Officers turned out, but interest died down enough for me to go to church and finish lunch before a fresh crowd gathered inside the wire - I joined it - of course! - and was just in time to see three figures in overalls follow each other out onto the skyline. We raised a cheer and a storm of clapping and as each one came up he saluted and bowed and showed every sign of excited delight. Imagine our surprise when the last turned out to be the Security Officer! He tore off his cap, smiled, bowed and ran down to the wire to say "What wonderful work! Why did only 26 go out?" and various other congratulatory comments that I couldn't quite follow.

In a word - good feeling all round - and nobody making any fuss beyond a formal search in the blocks against the wire to make certain there were no other tunnels still to be discovered. I think they were disappointed at finding nothing more.

So far then, all is very gentlemanly. It remains to be seen if Monday won't be more active.

A great show, Bertie, and you deserve success. We hope you'll have it, and never see this description. But if anything goes wrong I know you'll be amused to get something of the other side of the picture. It remains a great show - as M.G.M. would say, a sensation, and like all sensations, the Public loves it."

Vincent

By the way Colonel Tod was the Senior British Officer at the time, and Major Brush a Company Commander.

The reactions of the Germans seem to have been unexpectedly restrained. Gommell, who was a German Officer whom one most often saw in the camp, is said to have been boasting that our escape brought to Germany the record of the number of prisoners to get away from a tunnel. It had apparently previously been held by Britain for an escape by German prisoners from Donnington Hall in the First World War! He did have a sense of humour.

I cannot recall in detail the events of the next few days. We walked by night and lay up by day, and intended not to be seen, since neither our battle dress nor our German would stand inspection. We had chosen a dark night to break the tunnel, of necessity. We soon found that walking through woods or any rough country was unbearably tiring and dangerous. On one occasion I sat down on what seemed to be a trunk of a tree; it was in fact a hole in the ground several feet deep. No doubt David was surprised at my disappearing act and helped me out of the hole with some anxiety. Fortunately I had no injuries. I chose a good stick to probe such things in future. On another occasion I stepped into a pool, quite deep, on high ground. I had to sleep in wet clothes in the cold early morning. The compensation came at dawn when the sun rose, and the mountains of Austria and Switzerland were disclosed in all their fresh beauty.

Since we were so late out of the tunnel we decided not to go directly for Switzerland, as we should be likely to be picked up in the early days, but went more or less at right angles to the direct route; I should explain that one great barrier to reaching freedom was the river Rhine. There is however a salient of Switzerland, known as the Schaffhausen Salient, which extends over the Rhine and is therefore the favourite goal for escapers, well guarded though the crossing of the frontier there is. We decided however to take a route to the east, coming first of all to Austria, and then to try to cross into Switzerland by one of the passes there, or if the weather made this too hazardous, to seek our fortune in Liechtenstein. The problem about that alternative was that we did not know whether we should find sanctuary there, or would be turned back into Germany.

Our maps were rather primitive. They were made by tracing in copying ink maps which were obtained from the Germans by illicit means; the copies were then made by pressing the tracing on to jelly - the concentrated type that occasionally came in Red Cross parcels - and then running copies off the jelly. We had a compass of sorts, made by rubbing a razor blade on a magnet which one prisoner had, and pivoting it on a pin stuck through the bottom of a Gibbs Dentifice box. This should have worked, but ours was temperamental, and we marched mostly by the stars. As we were going more or less south most of the time we had to find a star which was at the other end of the night sky from the pole star, and walk towards that.

Our rations were what we carried. We had budgeted for about 30 days - we had a daily ration of one small bar of chocolate, a quarter of a cake made of oats, treacle, milk powder and margarine, baked hard, and one segment of cheese. This was not really enough to sustain our activity, so we lost weight; unfortunately after a stay in hospital and poor rations in that early part of the war I did not have much weight to lose, and we did not manage a great distance each night, perhaps 10 miles only, The other problem was that our feet were not equal to the additional strain on them. We had spent much time tunnelling, and in any case we had not been able to do much walking and certainly had not practised carrying the loads that our food supplies provided for us. I suffered dropped transverse arches, and we both, I think had strained Achilles tendons. Apart from that we made reasonable progress.

Memory of details of our journey has been clouded over and I did not make notes which might be read by Germans. Much of what Pat Reid describes in the early part of "The Colditz Story" applied to us also. One incident that remains clear is of a sunny day when we were lying in a small coppice and could hear the chiming of cowbells in the meadows of the hill opposite and see the shepherds peacefully at their work.

So we took the best way we could, avoiding villages where possible by making our way around them, though I remember we did set the dogs barking in one village but were not spotted. Our map was sufficient to guide us between Leutkirch and Memmingen, Kempten and Isny as we kept off the main road as far as possible, and on the seventh night after our departure from the camp we set off to walk up the valley of the River Iller, hoping that by the next day we should be in Austria. This would have been far from the end of our journey, but it would have been a psychological boost and we hoped that the population might be a trifle friendlier if we unfortunately came into contact with them. We had first to cross the watershed at the top of the valley and go along the Lechtal or Walsertal before deciding on our next objective.

It was the Iller that was our downfall. The river ran through flat countryside about a quarter of a mile wide, with steep thickly wooded hills rising up on either side, with a road running alongside the river. It would have been very tiring to move at night through the woods, so we set off across the flat lands alongside the road. We found however, that this was divided up into fields whose boundaries were drainage ditches and barbed wire. Negotiating these every hundred yards or so became exhausting, and our progress was extremely show, and we decided to accept the risk of going along the road until the terrain became easier. Unfortunately we found ourselves entering a small town - Sonthofen - which on our map was shown as off the road on our left. Still more unfortunately we came opon the town at about midnight just after a troop train had discharged its troops, and we were spotted by a railwayman and unable to bluff our way out. We were taken to a police house, I think it must have been, for the night, and returned to the camp at Biberach the next day.

So our personal adventure ended in failure. The endeavours over months of tunnelling had however borne much fruit. Three escapers from that tunnel made their way into Switzerland, and, as with all other escapes which had immediate success, the morale of the camp got a shot in the arm which nothing else but some allied victory could give; moreover for those of us who were recaptured we had, as it were, exorcised the feeling of guilt or inadequacy which our capture had injected into us. It was something to have broken out of the cage and lived on our own for seven days in a sort of freedom, and I think we were, as a result, more content with our lot. Bill Mercer got almost to the Swiss border before being recaptured.

As far as I was concerned I realised that my fallen arches made me unfit for long marches with heavy packs and if I got out again I should have to travel by other means.

Biberach was rich soil for other ways of escape. Officers disappeared through the gates in bundles of washing and in the rubbish cart. The Germans also provided a rather obvious means of escape in the situation of the bath house. For some unknown reason it was just outside the main gate, and when we went for our fortnightly showers we walked out past the guard on the gate, turned sharp left and into the bath house. There were two guards posted to see that we did not just walk off. If, however, two would-be escapers went into the bathroom and, instead of getting ready for the shower, donned blue coloured overalls as used by the German workmen inside and outside the camp, while they were hidden to view by the bodies of their companions, they might then walk out of the bath house door, past the guards and on into the area of the German Administration Block, from which they could easily escape. This was a simple enough procedure. The overalls were made out of pyjamas coloured with blue ink and were carried into the bath house in towels. The escapers worked in pairs, and over the weeks about four pairs must have got out of the camp in this way to the bewilderment of the guards. On one day however it was clear that a rat had been smelt, for there were three guards on duty, headed by a corporal. The pair who had planned to escape must have given little for their chances, but as luck had it they found that a ladder had been left in the changing room, so when they went out they carried this with them - and they walked straight past the guards in the usual way. By these and other devices five or six people got over to Switzerland from Biberach in the three months or so we were there, quite an achievement.

I spent three days in solitary confinement at Biberach, but my "punishment" for attempted escaping of ten days was interrupted by our move to Warburg near Kassel in the autumn of 1941. In due course I spent seven happy days in the cells there as I have already recounted.

Escaping. Warburg and Eichstätt.

Warburg proved to have many and varied opportunities for escape. As far as I was concerned my only involvement in an escape attempt, that is in which I myself would leave the camp, was another tunnel. I did not participate in the digging, which was from underneath a hut, but concentrated on disposal of the spoil. Outside our hut we had a fairly large flower bed which I tended. I did my gardening in the cool of the evening when the light was not too good, and the days spoil was delivered to me. I could not of course just put it on top of the top soil, as it was a different colour, so this had to be removed and the spoil inserted and the topsoil returned. As the flowers and plants grew this entailed careful transplanting. Somehow or another they survived the periodic shock to their systems, but the bed became more and more raised above the ground level, in the end standing quite proud. Unfortunately the tunnel was discovered at the last moment and that was the end for all of us. Naturally it was a great disappointment after so much work by so many people; by this time we were provided with forged documents by the escape committee and the forgers had spent days to prepare them. One man, John Mansel, (known as Thomas Cook), spent long hours every day doing nothing but forging; he would even produce, by some magic, apparently typewritten letters on a company's embossed letter heading to go with the papers. I was to be a French worker returning home on compassionate leave as my mother was said to be ill. The permission to travel and correspondence with my mother, including her photograph, and a letter from my employers were all there, and available if, as we travelled by train across the continent, we were interrogated. All this work by the devoted boys behind the scenes was wasted, on this occasion at any rate, so far as we were concerned. Incidentally, John Mansel's diaries which he kept during his imprisonment, recently published, give a vivid and true account of our reactions to our captivity and describe excellently our conditions in Thorn, Warburg and Eichstätt. I cannot set down here all the methods tried. There were the usual impromptu attempts to walk through the gate on one pretext or another. I do not think any of them had any success. In this camp there were a large number of R.A.F. Officers and it was interesting to notice a difference in attitude to escaping between the airmen and the army. The R.A.F. were eager to accept any opportunity which was offered to them at very short notice, and were good at short unplanned operations. The army on the other hand proceeded slowly with careful planning and slow deliberation. It was not that the R.A.F. did not do any tunnelling; a friend of mine named Hedley was continually tunnelling, now from one side of the hut and now from the other, then back again to the first side and so on as each tunnel was discovered in early stages. I saw him one day after his latest tunnel had been dug up by the German "Ferrets" who were often on the prowl with long crow bars to stick into the ground where a tunnel was suspected. I commiserated with him and enquired if he was going to give it up for a bit, and he replied, "Certainly not, one cannot allow oneself to get into a rut". He got home in the end I believe, repatriated for mental trouble - no doubt to some extent this was deception. One small Pole performed as a mole, that is he made a hole in the ground when no one was looking, and got the spoil away somewhere and when he had excavated sufficiently he got into the hole and made for the wire, packing the spoil behind him as he went. I do not remember, but cannot believe he made it. It sounds quite mad, but what courage!

One man whose whole object in life was escaping was Tom Stallard. He looked a bit like me, I suppose, and we planned at one stage to change places; I cannot remember why, but I think some of us were expecting to be sent to a different camp, and I believe for some reason he wanted, almost certainly for escape reasons, to stay in the camp and not be moved as was intended. However, as so often happened, the German plans were changed and we all left for Eichstätt, and no exchange of personalities was necessary. Tom used to spend most of his time watching the wire and the guards to find some weakness in their defences. There were two plans which were conceived by him. One was a direct attack on the wire by day, by himself and another with wire cutters. Someone had established that once one was under the wire one could not be seen, and could take time to cut through the aprons and crawl through the coiled barbed wire between them. The problem was to get in under the wire while the goons in the goonboxes were looking elsewhere. Diversions had therefore to be arranged, and near one of the goonboxes Douglas Bader and a companion were to be seen wandering round the perimeter, apparently in heated argument. When they had gone beyond the goonbox the companion gave Bader a shove and he fell down and both his legs came off. No doubt this developed into a lot of "business" while Tom Stallard and his friend, armed with wire cutters and pegs to hold up the coiled barbed wire, worked their way through and away. At the other end we started a controlled fire in a hut producing volumes of smoke, but no danger. The hole made by Tom was successfully used again later, and more diversions laid on. My recollection is that at our end on that occasion we resorted to noise, and no doubt produced a huge cacophony of shouts and bangings and clatter.

The biggest escape from this camp was an assault on the wire, again devised by Tom, but this time the escape was to be over it, and not through it. Someone had discovered that the perimeter lights, that is the lights hanging over the wire and illuminating it by night, could be fused from inside the camp. A trial run was carried out during a thunderstorm so that the Germans would think that the system had been struck by lightning. It worked, and the need was to make the best use of our ability to create sudden darkness. Tom's ambitious plan was to build four scaling ladders made of wood, tall enough to top the overhanging part of the wire apron, with another ladder pivoted to it to fold over and span the gap between the two aprons, and with rails to hold on to in the crossing and then drop down on the far side. Putting this plan into practice was a considerable undertaking. One day a gang managed to get into an unused wooden hut and, by dismantling much of the inner walling, to produce all the wood that was needed, and this wood, and the ladders as they were built, were used as shelving in the library. When the ladders were all ready, a dress rehearsal was held in the bath house. It was all done so discreetly that I do not think anyone would have known what was happening if he had not been in the know, or had drawn a correct conclusion from some "significant" action he had happened to see.

The library where the ladders waited for action was one of two blocks quite close to the wire, and happily the space between them was midway between two goonboxes. At night, in addition to the sentries in the goonboxes, there were two others who patrolled outside the wire, meeting at the front where the ladders were to be deployed and going back to a point underneath the goonboxes. It was essential therefore that both these sentries should have reached the limit of their beat, under the goonboxes, when the signal to start operations was given. I was one of two "stooges", looking as unconcerned as might be, who would give a signal to the officer in charge of the operation, Major Cousins, when our sentries were up to the end of their patrol. I was also to act as aide to Major Cousins when the fun began. There were reinforcements. At each end, near the goonboxes, stood a man with a grappling iron, who was to throw it into the wire when the lights went out, and start pulling as though there was to be an attack on the wire at that point. There were also to be two German speaking officers who would shout to the sentries outside the wire to stay where they were and guard that bit of the wire.

So the plans were laid and the 30th August, when there would be no moon, was chosen for the escape attempt. Having explained what was intended I will refer to two other large escapes which were to be synchronized with the ladder escape; it was hoped to create confusion in the German Kommandantur by this substantial evacuation. The first was a tunnel, a very large one at the other end of the camp. As I was not in it, though I knew of its existence, I did not enquire about it, as was one's way. I do not think I knew who was on it. The other was ingenious. When a tunnel or escape was discovered it was the habit of the Germans to send a squad of troops into the camp. A number of British Officers therefore, over the months, made for themselves with help throughout the camp, German uniforms and dummy rifles so that soon after the entry of the Germans they could march out impersonating the originals, leaving them to carry out their duties in the camp. I remember embroidering a number of German Eagles to be sewn onto the German Tunics made from blankets.

So the day of the exodus approached in September 1942, but a tragedy had happened some short time before when the young Scotsman was electrocuted while working at the face, as I have already described. His death was a great shock to everybody, and of course the tunnel failed, and the chance of making a spectacular series of operations had gone with it.

We came to the appointed day. The weather was right and those who were to escape collected in the library and the adjacent hut, and the rest of us went to our stations. Night had fallen by ten which I believe was zero hour. All was quiet and normal in the warmth of the late summer. The lights over the wire had been on for some time and the German Sentries were chatting opposite the space between the huts. At last they stopped talking, turned and walked away from each other. My sentry took his time but at length reached the end of his beat, and I gave the signal that the coast was clear at my end. Immediately the lights went out all over the camp perimeter. I ran to the point between the huts from which Major Cousins was directing the operation; the ladders were being run up to the wire and in a very short time one could see men going over them like ants over sticks, silhouetted against the sky. I think this must have been the most exciting moment of my life, but it could not last. The Germans started firing and the exercise was called off. Nobody was hurt in the shooting except, it was rumoured, two sentries who shot each other. Twenty six had escaped on these ladders; the R.A.F. one had not got into position - I believe they had not taken part in the dress rehearsal - and only a few men got over another ladder before it toppled out of alignment. Three of those escaping got back to England, after adventures some of which are told in a book called "Return Journey".

Unfortunately the Germans did not react in characteristic fashion and no squad of men entered the camp to investigate. It might well have been different if the tunnel had also broken, but it made impossible the escape by the British dressed as goons. Vincent Hollom was one of those who were to go out in this party; he had spent time in making dummy rifles and this was a great disappointment. Nevertheless it had altogether been a fine effort on the part of many people in the camp, with its tragedies and its disappointments but with its triumphs too.

So about a month later we were moved to Eichstätt, and took stock of our surroundings. We were told it was escape proof, which was a stimulating thought. Tunnelling was "ganz unmöglich" they said. I have described the camp already with the long lagerstrasse running the length of the camp from the main gate leading from the German administration block to the gate at the other end, very seldom used. Near the second gate was the hospital block with the dentists' surgery in it, and one of the very few occasions when this gate was used was when French prisoners came in to have their teeth seen to by our dentists. Incidentally the officials of the Protecting Power, by this time the Swiss, used to come to have their teeth seen to by our dentists, since we had, apparently, the best amalgam in Europe. Some escaping observer - it sounds like Tom Stallard - noticed that when these Frenchmen were marched in under a guard of two Germans, no passes were produced to the sentry on the gate, nor when they were marched out. It was planned that a posse of British, disguised as French prisoners and as two German guards, should walk out of this gate soon after a change of sentries, when the fact that no similar body had come into the camp wouldn't be noticed. It was of course important that their marching through the gates should not provoke any suspicion, and one step that was taken to prevent this was to make sure that no Germans were in the camp at the time. I was asked to ensure this.

I have mentioned that a number of prisoners escaped from Biberach by walking out of the bath building disguised only by putting on blue overalls. I was reminded of this, and my amusement and scorn, perhaps, at lack of alertness which permitted this, in the course of the Eichstätt escape. I had arranged stooges around the camp who gave me a signal when their areas were clear. I stood outside the hospital block and in due course gave the signal that the whole camp was clear. Almost at once I was horrified to see a German Unteroffizier coming out of this very block. How could I possibly have missed him? A moment later, of course, he was followed by a lot of French prisoners, and I realised that, even though I knew that this was just what I was expecting to happen, I was deceived momentarily by seeing someone in familiar guise doing some normal act. The sentry, I am glad to say, was equally deceived and they all got out, and two of them reached the Swiss border before being picked up. The same gate was later used in a similar escape but higher powered. A party consisting of a German General and his large and splendid entourage - all bogus - walked out of the gate and down the road. Unfortunately the sentry, though he had no suspicion that all was not what it seemed, rang through to the Kommandantur to report that the General had just left the camp. Consternation in the Officers mess with the buckling on of swords and straightening up, before the truth dawned on them! I do not think anyone got far.

One day I was sitting out in the sun reading when Hector Christie came and joined me; he had been busy on the tunnel from the abort at Biberach. He told me something of a tunnel which was being driven from one of the brick blocks along the Lagerstrasse, Block II. He said that he was looking for someone small, used to tunnelling and with good hearing and eyesight to act as an "outside stooge", that is to go up the tunnel with the director of the escape Frank Weldon who would actually make the break. The outside stooge would then take up a position in the hole alongside the break out point and police the traffic from there, covering up the hole roughly, before returning to the camp. Would I do it? Of course I agreed, but asked to see the tunnel as soon as possible.

It was to be a big affair, with 60 or so people going through it. It was exciting to be going down a tunnel again, but what a different exercise from our early efforts at Biberach! There was in this camp no trouble of disposal of the spoil, which could be either under huts at the far end of the camp or dribbled happily down the trouser leg. The tunnel therefore seemed to me very spacious; it was easy to get along on hands and knees. Nor was ventilation a problem as a chimney in one of the rooms was used to provide a draught, and the electric light was well organized. There were one or two big boulders to be squirmed round or under but otherwise it was plain going. There were several weeks work yet to go before the point outside the wire was reached where the break was to be made, but I had confidence in this tunnel from the start. It was being very well organised. The entrance, incidentally, was from under a W.C. which had to be moved to admit the working shift, but it was then closed down and the W.C. replaced, so good was the air supply.

So we waited. The only preparation I could make was one which I had taken at the beginning of the war, namely staying out in the dark to improve my night sight.

At last, after long weeks of waiting, the tunnel was ready to go. The weather was crucial. We had to have a moonless night but with wind to mask the sounds that would inevitably be caused as the escapers climbed out of the hole and up the hill away from the camp. The first date when there would be no moon was the 3rd May 1943, and all was ready for that day.

The 3rd was unsuitable as there was no wind; on the 4th there was a light breeze and it was decided to get the operation going, as far as actually opening and filling the tunnel with hopeful escapers, and then to await further news on the weather before making the break. Frank Weldon, who later commanded the King's Troop R.A.

and won an Olympic Gold Medal for Equestrian trials, and I crawled up the tunnel, with all those early on the list of escapers in the tunnel behind us. I lay alongside Frank, below where the opening would be from which I should act as lookout and direct the operations once Frank was out. So we lay there, almost in silence, and waited.

At last the message came up from mouth to mouth to the effect that the wind had dropped and it was left to Frank to decide whether to go on or not. I could picture his questions; would it be safe to move without the covering wind? On the other hand if we delayed and no suitable night occurred until the moon made it impossible, we should have to wait until the 23rd May for another chance, and by then the nights would be shorter, and all the time there was the risk that the ferrets might find the tunnel and all be lost. So we waited for what seemed ages; never have I felt the physical impact of concentrated thought as I did at that moment. In the darkness, and the confined space and in my nearness to Frank, his wrestling with his problem was palpable. After minutes, or tens of minutes, I do not know, he said quietly, "We go back". The operation went into reverse and eventually we crawled out into the light of the abort and faced the night.

Most of us at any rate were from different blocks, and we could not at this hour return to our own beds. Dummies were occupying them! In the attics of Block II there were on each side of the building areas under the eaves walled off from the living area. These walls had been breeched so that we could get into them; on one side was "Big Henry", a hide for men, and on the other side "Little Henry" where the baggage was stowed. So we all crammed into Big Henry, and spent a long and freezing night in the silence that the possibility of searching Goons demanded. It had been a very useful and successful exercise, but a great disappointment in many ways. The next days were equally unsuitable, and the operation had to be postponed until the 23rd May when the moon was again negligible. Would the tunnel be safe until then?

We returned to our occupations to find what tranquillity we could find there. On the 6th May however an extraordinary thing happened. Someone pinned a note to the lavatory door adjoining the room of the Senior British Officer with, written on it in capital letters, a sentence saying that the German Security Staff knew that we intended to break a tunnel in Block II and to prevent a loss of life we should not use it. The note was signed, "A German friendly to the British". On the following morning another note was found on the door of the abort of Block III in similar vein, but adding that a German patrol was waiting for us on the hillside. The question of course was whether this was genuine, written by a German as stated, or by some prisoner who was for some reason antagonistic to escaping, or some attempt at a joke. A watch was kept on the hillside so far as we could, and no sign of a patrol was seen. A decision had to be made on whether to go on with the attempt or abandon it. The Escape Committee resolved to go ahead but to decide at the last moment on the date and not to give the green light until after Appel in the evening. All the intending escapers and I were given the chance to withdraw, but none of us did. Again we waited on the weather.

The 23rd May came, and windless nights succeeded one another. Tension mounted. On the 26th it was decided to go before the 4th June, regardless. The plan was slightly altered, as it would not be dark until about 10.p.m. I must explain that outside the perimeter wire was a strip of grass and then a wood fence, and beyond that was the road, patrolled by a sentry, then another grass verge and a small bank with another wooden slatted, but not close, boarded fence on top of it. Some twelve feet behind that stood a wooden building, a hen coop or something of the sort and the exit hole was to be between the last mentioned fence and the building; beyond this was yet another fence. The first two out, Frank Weldon and Hamilton Baillie, were now to move in the dying daylight from the break hole to behind the building, guided by a signal from the attic, where there was a stooge who could see the road, that all was clear. They would then make a hole in the fence behind the building, laying a guide line to it and then beyond. When the hole in this fence was made, a signal was to be given to the attic and a signal sent to me at the exit hole so that the evacuation could start. One of the next out was to be the last man on the list. He was to stay near the building and direct the escapers to the hole in the far fence, and then, after all had gone, to gather up the guide ropes and be on his way.

The days went on, with clear and windless nights. The 3rd June passed. At Appel on the 3rd there was a towel in a certain window of Block III, and that alerted the stooges that the operation was on. Those who were on the escaping list were informed later - so strict was the security. I changed as inconspicuously as possible and went to Block II to go up the tunnel for the last time. We knew it was now or never. Frank Weldon broke through the turf forming the roof, and the fresh air flooded in. The exit was just where it was intended, and we packed the top soil away and prepared a place for me alongside the main exit, where I could look out on to the road and back into the camp. We then whispered goodbye to each other, and he and Hamilton Baillie moved out on signal from the Block III attic and crept up behind the hut. I took up my position and awaited events.

The wind had dropped, but thank heavens the crickets were chirping their hearts out, and the noise they made was almost deafening. My view of the road was restricted by the slats of the fence and some bits of vegetation among them, and I was forced to rely very much on my hearing to locate the guard on his beat. I had two signals to help me, operated from inside the block on the instruction of the stooge in the attic who had some view of the road. One was a dim electric light in the tunnel which shone when the coast was clear, and as a standby in case this should fail a signal operated by a cord.

It was not too long before the light came on to show that the hole in the wire behind the hut had been made, and I could start the evacuation. I found I could keep up quite a good flow as the men crawled up to the hole alongside me and climbed out and went up the bank to the stooge by the hut. There were of course hitches, packs had come adrift as they were pushed through the tunnel; one man seemed to find some corrugated iron to tread on as he went up the hill, and I had to hold everything to see how the guards were reacting. Unbelievably they seemed to ignore it. Then later I saw the light go out, and again had to hold everything, though I did not from my position notice anything untoward. Long minutes passed and I began to worry about the men in the tunnel where the air could not be very good. I waited for a signal on the cord system, thinking the electric wiring might be broken, but no signal came. There must be some trouble I could not see or hear. At last a message came up the tunnel, from mouth to mouth, that both systems of signalling had failed, and I was on my own. We had wasted a lot of time, so I re-started the evacuation as quickly as I could, trusting as I must to my own observations. All went well, though as a French Canadian was getting out of the hole I noticed a guard approaching, and I held the man's leg and dug my fingers into his ankle. He froze with his face to the ground; in the meantime the guard was clearly suspicious and peered through the fence, but then, apparently satisfied, went again on his beat. Fortunately this was nearly at the end of the list and I was able to clear the tunnel of all the escapers, wishing them well as they went, before early dawn started to lighten the scene. I covered the hole up quite roughly so that it would not be too obvious before Appel - it was not intended to use it again - and came back into the block.

I do not remember anything of the rest of the night, but I cannot think that any of us on the "staff", "Sigs" Jackson, Tony Rolt, Hector Christie and Jack Hale and I slept during the rump that remained; as soon as we could move about the camp I returned to my room in Block I with interest in the coming events of the Appel.

It was a wonderfully warm morning, and we all went on parade with more than our usual books and other amusements in expectation of a long spell on the parade ground and we were not disappointed. The Germans established that there were 67 missing. (Of those, 65 had gone out through the tunnel, and two were ghosts; that is officers who from then on would not be on the strength of the camp, but might later on escape without the Germans being aware that they had only just done so and being alerted to look for them). Naturally the guards had first to find the tunnel - we may have shown them, I cannot remember - but I was quite happy to be out on the warm grass and make up lost sleep.

The scheme, apart from the signalling failure, had worked perfectly, and we had got 65 away. This was by far the biggest break up to that date, and the Germans apparently assumed that it was timed to coincide with the opening of a second front in the south of France and stood to over quite a large part of Europe. It has been said that it was a mistake to send out so large a number, as the Volksturm, the Home Guard, was called out which not only made it more difficult for the escapers - all of whom were later recaptured and sent to Colditz - but also that it gave a useful exercise to the Home Guard Units. We had however provided ample evidence that we could indeed escape by tunnels, and no doubt this tied up German troops to prevent a recurrence. As will be seen our next tunnel escape was for much smaller numbers, but this was for quite different reasons.

The 1943 second front was a mirage, and we had to return to our normal prison lives. It could not be expected that, now that the Germans' boast that tunnelling in the camp was "ganz unmöglich" had been proved so spectacularly wrong, restless spirits would not start on a fresh tunnel. It was I suppose, in the spring of 1944 - I do not recall the exact dates - that I was asked by one of the Escape Committee to do the same outside stooge's job as before for this new tunnel. It was more ambitious than the first in that it was much longer. It was being dug from the same block but instead of going at right angles to the wire it went out at an angle of about 45° and was to finish in a sort of kitchen garden opposite Block III, the administration block on the other side of the Lagerstrasse, and further along, so it was quite a length. The most difficult part of any tunnel was to hide the entrance from the prowling and probing "ferrets". This tunnel trap was ingenious. The staircases in Block II had, like most free standing staircases, a wooden backing so that the underneath reverse of the treads and risers of the stairs would not be in view. This wooden backing was removed and the tunnel entrance was underneath the bottom step of the staircase. The line of the backing was changed somewhat to give a little more room for the hole, but it was nevertheless very restricted and it was hard to insinuate oneself into it. It also demanded very good stooging so that it could be closed down quickly if a goon was anywhere near.

    I think the escape of 65 the previous year had upset the Germans more than we realized, as posters were put up telling us that escaping was a "damned dangerous act" and "no longer a sport". We took no notice of this. Then later we heard of the escape from Stalagluft, which was the subject of "The Great Escape", and the killing of so many of those who had got out through that tunnel. The war was by now surely coming to an end and the invasion of Normandy had already taken place by the time our tunnel was ready to go. It must have seemed to the Escape Committee that the risking of so many lives was not then justifiable. It was discovered moreover that if the number involved in any escape were kept below ten the local Kommandant did not have to inform The Higher Command. So the plans were changed; only eight were to go out on the night, but the hole was then to be closed as carefully as possible from the inside, in the hope that it would not be discovered and could be used on another night for another batch. This was explained to us all and again we were given the chance to withdraw, but did not do so. Incidentally, another note was found, similar to that at the time of the previous tunnel, but it was not treated quite so seriously as before; I do not know if anyone found out who had written it. The evacuation took place on the 18th June 1944.

    Whether it was because the Normandy landings and the subsequent battles were in the forefront of our minds and the tunnel in comparison was less important, or for some other reason I do not know, but my recollection of that operation is by no means as vivid as that of the previous one. As far as I was concerned all went well; I got the eight out according to plan, and another officer and I were closing the hole somewhat carefully when one of the escapers was spotted on the hillside. It was not long before most of them were caught though one was out for 3 months before recapture; nor was it long after we scrambled down the tunnel and back into the block that the ferrets followed in our tracks.

This was to be a short operation in any case and I was changing beds for most of the night with my distant cousin Brodie Cochrane, who lived in Block II. To his bed then I retired before things began to happen inside the camp. There was a snap parade that lasted from 2.30 - 4.00 a.m., quiet and peaceful - fortunately nobody had been hurt and there were no serious reprisals. It had not been a great success and it was fortunate that our expectations had on this occasion been smaller, and that the course of the war seemed to make attempts to escape less demanding.

I was of course delighted that those two assignments, which involved considerable responsibility, had, as far as I was concerned, gone off well. My delight was very largely in the fact that it was a credit to my regiment The Worcestershire Yeomanry - so strong was our regimental spirit, seldom expressed, and so great was the spur and power that it gave.

Eichstätt. Towards The End………

I cannot remember any more escape attempts, and our attention was more on the battle of France and the developments on the Eastern Front. I was reading Churchill's "Marlborough" at the time and I was struck by the similarity of Marlborough's tactics at Blenheim - and later battles - to Monty's tactics around Caen. In each case the British battered at the hard core of the enemy until the time was ripe and then the allies on the wings swung round to encircle the enemy. What seemed to many to be the setbacks and delay of the British advance seemed to me to be part of the plan, and the subsequent rapid advance by Patton's forces on the right wing substantiated this. Nevertheless the war dragged on and there were disappointments as in the failure of the Arnheim operation and the shock of the Germans' push in the Ardennes, though this looked as if it must be a final and despairing fling.

The conditions in the camp were somewhat eased. I will try to describe the room I was in for most of my time in Eichstätt, from the handcuffing episode onwards. We were thirteen of us, sleeping in two-decker beds. We were a mixed lot, for four of us were English, one Scottish, two Canadian, three Australians, two New Zealanders and one Rhodesian. We got on very well and I was reminded that only once was there anything approaching a quarrel and that was between the two New Zealanders who were very different characters. In such a confined space, where the smallest thing, like a little mannerism or a repeated turn of phrase, could jangle the nerves in an unbelievable way, this was quite an achievement. By this time games and logging parties and parole walks were becoming more common and permitted a change of view which was very valuable. Nevertheless some relationships were becoming a bit frayed; perhaps the prospect of the end of the war helped to loosen our ties with each other and upset the routines which we had managed to establish. Our eyes were being lifted to fields, beyond the camp and indeed Germany, where we no longer had common ground.

One question which was a horizon to our thoughts was how the war would end. In fact a few of us were brought together at the insistance of the Senior British Officer to plan a physical takeover of the camp in certain circumstances, and a preliminary scheme was prepared to this end; events however moved, before long, in other directions. This question was one which we were all asking and I remember well being asked by Phil Dennison, who was one of my law "pupils", to go for a walk with him. This was a common practice when one wanted to have a serious discussion; as one walked round the perimeter one had comparative privacy, and the rhythm of walking makes conversation more relaxed. Phil Dennison was anxious to find out from me how I thought our prison life would come to an end. I told him what I thought might happen, and probably had in mind that the Americans would surround the camp in force and that the Germans would surrender it without any serious opposition and that in due course we should be transported home. That seemed the straightforward expectation We discussed the possibilities at length, and I remember Phil saying something like "I'm sorry, but I just cannot see going home". I will refer to this again later.

Air activity was more and more frequent as the Allies approached. On one occasion when a daylight raid was in progress and we were confined to our barrack blocks one officer went out of his hut to have a look at the planes. He was promptly shot by the sentry. A friend jumped out to tend to him and he again was shot - both were killed. The name of the guard was discovered, I believe, and he came up before a war crimes court. It was a black day for the camp.

It was about this time, I think, that news reached the Senior British Officer - how I do not know - that a German informer was being introduced into the camp. Plans were made that if this were to happen he would be kept under the closest surveillance for every minute of the day and night. The Germans were told of this, and warned that the S.B.O. would not be responsible for his safety if he came into the camp. That was the last that was heard of this stool pigeon.

The air provided one surprise. Not very long before the end of the war some German planes came over, flying fast and low, and quite silently. The roar of the engines followed immediately afterwards. They were the first jet planes of the war I think, made in a factory not far from us. They were, I was told, rather unmanoeuverable, but it is fortunate that they came on the scene so late in the war.

For us the war dragged on. We had maps on the wall with flags showing the positions of the troops as divulged in the German papers; we could not of course disclose the fact that we had access to sources of news more favourable to the Allies. We made forecasts of the course of the fighting on the three fronts, Russian, French and Italian. I was generally more pessimistic than the rest, but nevertheless I was still far too optimistic; and at length we settled down to the fact that we should be spending yet another winter in Germany. Hope was continually being deferred, and we were becoming rather sick at heart. We became very introspective and at times morose. Depressions descended on us, and some even dreaded going home at the end of the war. My remedy for depressions which hit us in early days was to read a Jane Austen novel, and this never failed me. Later on in the war however I found many works such as Toynbee's Study of History not so much relaxing as stimulating, and that had the same effect. There were plenty of things to do, as I shall show, to balance the introspection. For some people however this was not so easy, and it was hard for others to do much for them; in particular the closeness of our relationships, in both senses, made it difficult to help anyone who at any one time was bottling things up. It seemed that we were forming, as at the beginning of our imprisonment, hard skins as a barrier against those we knew so well. I wonder if self doubts and jealousies are features of all closed communities.

I have notes of some happenings at this time. I had two weeks on the outside parole wood party. We went out under light guard and spent our days cutting up old tree stumps so that they could be got back into the camp. These weeks were very happy ones; the weather was very cold but the sun shone, and I recall still the smell of the wood fires and the cooking stew, and above all the quietness and serenity of it and the feeling that together we were engaged on some worthwhile and natural activity.

Of Christmas itself I wrote:-

"Then Christmas. Weather which I have never met before, I think, all this time, cold crisp sunny, with golden mornings and opalescent evenings when the blood almost began to rise. This you may say was enough to cheer the heart and raise the excitement, but in addition the Germans, by an order forbidding us to keep reserve parcels, have forced us to overeat, and we propose to go on doing so steadily until we get back to German rations in three weeks time. Our Christmas eating then was a success, porridge, eggs and bacon and sausage, toast and marmalade for breakfast, pilchards with mustard sauce for lunch, my own cake with almond icing and chocolate hard icing, nuts and caramel, was as good as I remember. Soup and roast Canadian meat roll, and too much very sickly Christmas pudding, also largely my work, lifted us very high in the scale of satiety. The whole thing, the weather food and season, combined to create a friendly atmosphere we have not had for a long time".

It will be seen how much our minds were on food, and I must recount the saga of "my own cake". I had some weeks before Christmas decided that this must be our last in prison and that it merited something which resembled a Christmas cake. We had no flour or eggs or baking powder, so we used what we had; biscuit crumbs and rye bread crumbs and millet, carrots and dried fruit of some kind, a tinned marmalade pudding laced with beer - that sort of thing. I wanted to lighten it a bit, so I incorporated a German equivalent of Eno's which one could get in the canteen. That should do the trick, I thought, as I worked the mixture into the cake tin and gave it to the cook sergeant to put into the communal oven in the cookhouse. It exceeded my expectations. As I was reading the German papers that afternoon the sergeant came in and said "Please sir, what am I to do with your cake?" I asked for more information and he said "It's all over the floor of the oven". I handed him a cardboard box, and asked him to scrape it all off the floor of the oven and bring it back to me in the box, together with the cake tin - this of course as if it was all part of the masterplan and entirely expected. In due course a box full of crumbs, and no doubt other debris from the bottom of the oven, arrived with the cake tin and some remains still in it; I pressed it all back into the tin and asked the sergeant to return it to the oven. In the event it was a very good cake. Whatever we may say of the ingredients, the method is a little complicated for me to recommend it for normal application!

I have written as though our food depended entirely on the German rations and food parcels, mostly from the Red Cross. This was not entirely so; there was quite a lot going on under the counter in these later days. Cigarettes had become a valuable commodity in the closing stages of the war, and the Black Market was active. So serious did it become that the Kommandant appointed a German N.C.O. to put an end to it. It was unsuccessful, since soon afterwards we persuaded Nancy, as he was called, to bring into the camp a large pike, which we ate with more relish and appreciation than it normally enjoys. Better still, for a large number of cigarettes, and in fear and trembling, he brought in a whole lamb's carcase under his cape. There was also on one occasion food from heaven. A goose was in its own prison camp a little up the hill, and it planned an escape. It took to its wings and flew over its perimeter wire and somewhat overdid it by flying over our wire as well. That was a mistake, for by the time a guard came to find it, the poor bird was dead, plucked and dressed, and was cooking merrily in some Aussie's oven. Escaping can be dangerous. On a lower plane there was an occasional addition to be grasped by the quick witted. The rubbish carts, including the carts taking the sewage out of the camp, were usually pulled by oxen. On one or two occasions they were pulled by cows in milk. On these occasions the workman would be engaged in interesting conversation and when he returned to his job, the cow would be dry. The garden on the lower part of the camp, devoted to the growing of fresh vegetables, also provided a valuable addition to our diet.

My days were full, thank heavens. Three weeks on wood stumping, some parole walks either in the country-side or the interesting town of Eichstätt, and various sports, basket ball or five-a-side hockey and cricket, and in the winter skating on an improvised rink. Then I was doing Divorce with Fitz Fletcher and Dick Troughton, both of whom got firsts in the exams, and the latter a double first and a congratulatory letter from the Lord Chief Justice; I also discussed divorce papers with John Peyton - later in Edward Heath's cabinet - and Tort with David Stebbings. My normal day might include tennis at 7, reading till lunch, then basket ball, preparing an evening meal and law in the evening. My reading was of serious stuff, and it was Toynbees' Study of History and Whiteheads philosophical books which I found most stimulating, but I read a great many books during the years. I have forgotten most of them but perhaps they are still locked into the subconscious.

It will be seen that there were at Eichstätt opportunities for a number of sports. I have mentioned tennis and basket ball; we also had a five-a-side hockey which was played during the summer on an ice hockey pitch, a fast and exciting game as the ball never went out of play. We did not of course have suitable "strip" for the team games, so the differentiations was between "shirts" and "skins". There was also baseball - mostly softball - and cricket, which surprisingly often worked up to a thrilling finish in the last over of the match. At Warburg we had been allowed sabres for fencing - on parole - but after a week or so the Germans thought better of it and the sabres were withdrawn.

I spent some time during this period digging in the garden or sawing wood, and later on in sharpening saws etc. I also did some book-binding under Jumbo Burrough and found this most rewarding. Then there were concerts and plays, and we had some films to see - even, somehow, a Fred Astaire and Ginger Rogers one. On a Sunday I would usually go to a Church of Scotland Service, as this seemed more suitable to a hall regularly used for plays etc. the C of E Communion seemed to me out of place there. There were lectures from time to time and we paid each other visits and went for walks round the perimeter, from which often a train of thought might arise to excite the imagination for some days. One's enthusiasm at this stage of the war needed continually to be stoked with fresh stimuli. There were more restful pursuits. I had been sent a Carnel crotchet hook which I had used before the war and have used ever since. With this I crocheted 7 blankets for nationals of a number of countries. The wool of course could not be bought, but it came from old pullovers or socks which were no longer serviceable. Roger Mortimer, who later was Racing Correspondent with the Sunday Times, would undertake knitting on large gauge needles, to knit a full size sleeved pullover in the course of a day. I also used to crotchet the crown of a "Chasseur Alpin" type of hat, with others providing the knitted sides and woven peak. One of these we made for John Elphinstone, the Queen's cousin.

It was with some apprehension that we entered 1945. Much was now happening. There were continued rumours of repatriation of the grands blesses. There was an excellent performance of Comedy of Errors, to which I went twice. It was produced by Michael Goodliffe. My 33rd birthday was celebrated by the Germans by their removal, as a reprisal for something or another, of our mattresses and stools and tables. It was childish, and provoked more laughs than anger. We thought the Nazis were expecting great success for their Ardennes offensive and that this had brought on a return to their "success" treatment; we knew however, by this time from our own radio, that the push had failed. We were, by March, seeing low flying allied aircraft over the valley, and the Red Cross parcels had run out and the German rations cut. The end of March was outwardly calm, but there was talk of a move and counter rumours that the Kommandant intended to surrender us to the Americans when they came. The future was obscure, but there was an end of term feeling in the air.

With April the tension rose. A number of senior officers who had been taken to another camp returned unexpectedly, and one of them was obsessed with conditions in Munich - its desolation, and its inhabitants sleeping in the trams and dying of malnutrition, though doctors were forbidden to give this as a cause of death. Compared with them we were very lucky - I note that we entertained one of the returning officers to steak and kidney pudding, potatoes and fried turnips, apricots and semolina pudding and egg savoury. Our minds were still much on food.

Armoured vehicles by this time were from time to time seen going along the road. I started the month on a wood party and found there in the forest peace and relaxation, but as we returned to the camp our excitement grew to find out what developments had taken place in our absence, whether the growing imminence of a move or an influx of prisoners from other camps. Even in the forest there was some tension, but on the part of German civilians one might meet. There was fear of the arrival of the Americans, who, I tried to explain, were not all black savages. On one day there was a ferocious air raid, apparently on Ingolstadt. As the raid subsided a woman and her young son came into the wood - they had, it seemed, been in an earlier raid there and both were jittery, and it was horrid to see the child run screaming into the wood at the sound of a plane. So many of the civilians kept saying that they were not responsible - it was the worst government anyone had ever had, or just fate. It was odd for someone in my position, though it seemed natural enough, to be comforting German civilians as much as one could, advising them to stay put and not to run before the storm, and trying to give them hope for the future. They all seemed to expect another war to start fairly soon, between the Americans and the Russians, and to be resigned to it. "Mankind is so foolish" they said, and expected their children to be just as bad. Their children, by the way, seemed also to seek the reassurance that the prisoners gave them. Later on one heard the cry of "Es gibt Hungersnot" - there is famine - as though some folk memory of the Thirty Years War was surfacing from the murky seas of the "folk subconscious".

Back in the camp we were still being

threatened with a move. It seems that Hitler had decided to move as many prisoners as possible to a "Southern Redoubt" where we could be used as hostages to secure good terms from the Allies in peace negotiations. Naturally our senior officers were trying to stall and play for time, hoping that the Americans might make a sudden dart in our direction. But we were busy packing, making rucksacks out of old battle dress jackets and small carts to enable us to carry more goods with us. There was a bit of a flap on.

The Last Days

We were justified in our fears, for on the 14th April we moved out on to the road just outside the camp. We were in a holiday mood, and must have looked an odd collection, some thousand odd of us pulling extra- ordinary constructions to carry our goods and chattels on the journey into the unknown. At any rate we were leaving the camp which had held us for so long. The townspeople were sorry to see us go; while we were there they thought the Allies would not bomb the town, and their future suddenly became more insecure. So there we were waiting for the instructions to start the march. The sun was out and six allied planes, Thunderbolts, seemed to want to add to our enjoyment by flying low down the railway on the other side of the valley, dropping bombs on the track and giving us a grandstand view of their power; then they disappeared. More waiting and then suddenly out of the blue the allied planes returned, changed their direction and flew along the length of our column from a height of 200 to 300 feet with their machine guns blazing. So unexpected was this that we had not taken cover, and we were on the road or the side of it, but we quickly went to ground as best we could; I was in a quarry, lying low, and one prisoner lying alongside me tried, when the planes came over on a second wave, to get underneath me. I looked at his face; instead of being carefree and excited with the prospect, however full of danger it might be, of the march ahead of us, it was ashen with terror; I expect all our faces were much the same.

I believe 17 prisoners were killed and 70 injured in this attack. There are two stories to tell. One relates to some German children playing near the prisoners at the back of the column. When the machine- gunning started some of the prisoners got hold of the children and shielded them as best they could with their own bodies. The other is of one young prisoner who was hit by shots and fell. A German interpreter, who was near, carried him to a ditch and, amidst all the shooting, erected a pile of stones round his head to give some protection. Unfortunately he was one of those who died; he was Phil Dennison, who, as I have said earlier, was worried about how the war would end and did not see himself going home.

How can this have happened? There were we, a rabble army if ever there was one, just outside a prison camp, dressed all in khaki taking no evasive action at all. At the time we were under the impression that the planes were American and the pilots thought we were Axis troops, but decided not to drop bombs but to use machine guns, just in case we were Allied prisoners! The story I have now heard, however, is that the planes were flown by the Free French, and that they assumed, not knowing I suppose of the existence of the camp, and seeing that we did not have a white flag flying, that we were part of the Hungarian Army, easy meat for them. Hungary was the only Axis country which wore Khaki, and it was true that we had no white flag; we had told the Germans that we ought to have one but it was refused, so blame seems to be divided. Deaths in war are so often caused by mismanagement or stupidity.

The machine gunning went on for wave after wave, and Dick Tomes, Vincent Hollom and I, who had planned to leave the column with two others, if the opportunity presented itself, came to the conclusion that it would be better to be killed by the enemy than by our own side, so during a moment when the guards were taking cover from an attack we ran for the woods. There was some firing, but whether it was intended to do more than scare us I do not know, and another attack by the planes put the guards to ground again.

Dick Tomes, a regular soldier and a Godson of Montgomery, wrote his story shortly after the event, and I am quoting largely from it. He tells the tale far better than I can.

After reaching the woods, we sank down among the trees, exhausted and suffering from reaction. We opened our packs and jettisoned everything except what would be necessary for our attempt to reach the American lines. Then we went to the far side of the wood and hid up. D.T. says:-

> "We made a most welcome mug of tea on a Meta Stove and then just as we had finished it, we heard shouts of beaters calling to each other only a few hundred yards away. There was nothing for it but to lie as quietly as possible. This we did, hardly daring to breathe as they came closer and closer. Two German troops came up to the copse and then skirted it and were within ten yards of our hiding place. We heard them talking together about the absurdity of beating the forest and grumbling about the heat - then, miraculously another voice - presumably their N.C.O.'s - called, ordering them to swing over to the left and leave our part of the wood".

We settled down to sleep, but got up early

on the 15th April, walking from 5.a.m. to 8.a.m. when we found a reasonable hide for the day. The problem was water, and we were driven to fill our water bottles from cart ruts. In the evening we set off, keeping to the edge of the woods, in the direction of gunfire to the north west.

I remember that as we went along on this or a subsequent day we heard a loud cough from behind a hedge and froze. It was a sheep of course, but it sounded like an unrestrained human cough. We were puzzled too on one occasion by a "pink - pink" noise from close by, either a water ram or an electric fence no doubt.

Our only map was one on a pamphlet dropped by Allied planes, and this was not much help. On the 16th we found an excellent hide and heard our first cuckoo and gloried in the wild flowers - such a contrast to all the noise of gunfire and aircraft. In fact the gunfire was a bit too close as there was a German battery nearby. Because of this and the difficulty of finding water we set off again; finally, early next morning, we found an excellent hide, open to the sun but approachable only by crawling. Here we stayed for four days, going out every night to a good source of water about two miles away. I well remember on our return one night hearing a nightingale singing very happily in the tree immediately above us and being delighted one day by a goldcrest which visited the furze around us.

We had to decide what to do. Our food would not last long, and we might be hit by bad weather, though we had found a barn to shelter in if necessary. Should we do best to stay put and wait for the Americans, who seemed from the gunfire to be coming no nearer? Should we move on again towards the gunfire, or try to contact one of the foreign workers in the fields? We were suffering from inaction, and becoming bored and irritable. We made up our minds to move north westwards and as we came out into the open on the 20th April we could see the lurid glow of Nuremburg in flames. As we skirted a wood a strange thing happened. D.T. says:-

"We were all standing at the edge of a wood, but just inside, looking to see if it was safe to cross a road, when B.E. who was on the outside and almost in the open quickly lay down and whispered "Be quiet". Then across the field and only a few yards from us, four silent and stealthy figures approached the road. It was a bright moonlight night and we could see them plainly. They quickly glanced right and left and then crossed it and disappeared into the woods on the far side. After they had gone we realised that the chances were that they too were escaped prisoners, intent on not being seen and on getting to the American lines. We cursed ourselves for not realising this more quickly, accosting them and trying to get news, a map or some bread. However we went on, never expecting to see them again when we again heard them in the woods. It seemed that they were sitting down, hiding from us and about 100 yards away. We had a hasty, whispered consultation and decided it was worth risking - they were so obviously intent on not being seen and could not be Germans. So, spreading out, we walked slowly towards where we thought they were. B.E. walked right into them and addressed them in French, "Prisonniers de Guerre"? he whispered, "Oui" was the furtive reply. In a second we had put each

> other at ease - at least neither party was German.
>
> I came up a few seconds later and experienced a nasty moment when I saw what looked, in the shadows of the trees, remarkably like a German with a rifle and three huge tough men. As a matter of fact this was precisely what the party was, as we discovered after a short and whispered conversation in that eerie spot. Three Russian prisoners from a working commando were going off with their guard who was taking them to hide up at his home nearby to await the Americans, he himself being a deserter. We exchanged cigarettes for some large chunks of very stale and mouldy, but nevertheless very acceptable bread, and parted with handshakes and mutual good wishes. They could give us no news of the whereabouts of the Americans"

The next day was very rainy, and by 6.p.m. we were wet through, and felt we must get moving, although there were still some hours of daylight. We pressed on for about 6 hours in the driving rain. The rain stopped soon after midnight and we began looking for a barn. Dick notes:-

> "But before one could be found we were brought up short by a "Halt". An effort to bluff it out was unavailing. "Was Kompanie?" "Siebzehn" answered B.E. promptly. "Siebzehn? Keine Siebzehn - was sind sie? Amerikaner, wahr nicht!" No, we said, not Amerikaner and explained who we were.
>
> We were marched back by two men,

hands above our heads, to their platoon and then Battalion H.Q. in the town of Haideck. It was a walk of some two miles, but after a bit V.H. with his excellent German and amazing manner with the Germans had thawed our captors. He gave them some chocolate and cigarettes and they became chatty and told us the Americans were only 200 metres from the point where we were recaptured. This was news indeed - though infuriating. Thinking they were still miles off, we had not been on the look-out for infantry posts and had been easily able to avoid what few guns there seemed to be. The Americans had actually, we were told, been in possession of this very area during the day but had withdrawn at dusk. However, it also meant that with luck, if we could delay matters sufficiently, they would liberate us next day. In Battalion H.Q. - a beautifully warm Gasthaus - we were kept for a few minutes only, where a young orderly officer, very tired and irritable took down some particulars and sent us off to a barn where we slept with the troops. Soaked to the skin, weary and disappointed, we took off most of our clothes and getting into partially wet blankets lay on some straw, as close as we could get together for warmth.

For the remainder of the night we were repeatedly trodden on as dead tired soldiers staggered in, or were dragged out to go on patrol or sentries cursing and grumbling. At first light the whole company fell

> in, having come to life, and inspected us with friendly curiosity, giving us bread for cigarettes and informing us that we would be free that day as the Americans were but a mile or so away, if not less. We were again taken to Battalion H.Q. where the whole staff was packing up preparatory to moving back."

We were marched out of Walling at 12.30 p.m. and managed, by delaying tactics, to take four hours over the journey to Enslingen. At the Division H.Q.:-

> "There was one amusing incident at Divisional H.Q. A conceited and self- important young Intelligence Staff Officer, thinking we were brand new prisoners picked up on the front and members of a new British Division operating with the Americans, came bustling along giving orders that we were to be closely watched in case we tried to destroy papers. Then going into a room he said he would interview me first and alone. He spoke good English and studying my cap he fired questions at me - What was my rank, unit, Brigade, Division, what papers had I? I produced the only 'papers' I had - a small wad of toilet paper and two little German booklets on wild flowers that I carried with me! "No! No! No! your papers, your identity card, orders etc." I mentioned then that we had been captured five years ago and were unlikely to be of much interest to him, and his face fell. To give him his due he laughed at his own

> mistake and admitted he thought he was on the track of a new and important troop movement of British Units to the South!
>
> After this we were left in a room with our sentry and the civilian owners of the house who, as previous ones had done, begged us to stay and make it all right for them when the Americans arrived. They were scared of the rough type of U.S.A. soldier molesting the girls and in particular of having negroes in the village. They were highly amused at the mistake of the German I.O. - a young Prussian whom they did not like having billetted on them and who obviously ordered them about, as we had seen, in an imperious manner".

So we were moved back towards Eichstätt, as slowly as we could persuade our guards to go. In one of our stops,

> "We spent an amusing hour in a cottage where the old Hausfrau made us some tea and cocoa which we supplied and handed round a large circle of evacuees, together with condensed milk for the children and cigarettes for the men. Sitting in a warm parlour amongst these simple friendly countryfolk was a strange and even exciting experience after so many years of never even seeing a proper room with a 'home' atmosphere."

So we returned to Eichstätt. Dick had a very nasty swollen foot, and was admitted to hospital. We were sad to part, but for him it was clearly the most sensible action, and his story from then on is different from ours, so different that I think it is worth quoting. He recalls that this hospital was full of badly injured Germans and also some of the British Officers injured in the air attack. The Germans, whether wounded or medical staff, did not know what had become of their homes and families; they faced the possible ruin of their country and they all might have to endure the bombing and annihilation of the town, but

> "the nursing sisters, doctors and orderlies were magnificent and worked like blacks with no discrimination and always a cheerful word for anyone. Most of the time was spent in the cellar or downstair passages and the tension was very trying, but it was great piece of character study to see how these Germans, terribly battered and ill as they were, and knowing that their country was completely finished, bore it. The general "Kamaradschaft" shown by everyone, no matter what nationality at a time when we might all have been blown to pieces was really rather a wonderful experience.
>
> The 'Battle of Eichstätt' was abortive and largely owing to a remarkable woman did not take place. The Nazi Burgermeister had decreed that the town would be defended to the last, and positions had been dug all round and the bridges blown. But he had more than the U.S Army to deal with. The Mother Abbess of the Convent, an imposing woman who was used to having her orders obeyed and who was the real power in that old

town of Convents and churches, said 'No'. The local Volksturm were with her and refused to blow the last bridge, a lovely old mediaeval one with statues of the old Prince Bishops. The leads were cut by two Volksturm who were caught by the S.S. and hanged publicly on a tree in front of the Cathedral; the bridge was then blown, destroying an old church and some houses and breaking glass everywhere. But the Mother Abbess sent spies through the German lines to tell the Americans that the town, full of hospitals of German, British and American sick and wounded and of monastries, convents churches and religious and historical relics would not, if she could help it, be defended, as she was negotiating with the local German Commander and hoped to persuade him to withdraw. This gained time, and she succeeded in her object.

By the evening of the 24th there were but a few Germans north of the town and all that night guns were firing across the valley and town, which were now virtually no-mans-land, the exits and entrances were being shelled by either side and some lumps of shrapnel came into our courtyard and through the roof, but the town was in the main untouched. That night, however, in the cellar, not knowing that the Germans were pulling out, was a tense and frightening one.

Next morning dawned with bright sunlight and at 10 O' clock someone rushed in to say that the white flag had been hoisted on the Cathedral Spire. This, as it turned out later, was also the Mother Abbess' orders. There was a moment's silence and then people broke down, wept or laughed hysterically. Some of us went up to the attic windows where we could see the flag and by this time other white flags were fluttering from windows and roofs all over the town.

A few minutes later an American reconnaissance patrol came into the town and passed down the road below us. I dared not speak for I knew I should burst into tears if I did.

We had been liberated, not by Gen. Patch at all, but by Gen. Patton's Army, who had beaten him to it and came in from the North East - The 86th (Blackhawk) Division of the 3rd Corps of the 3rd Army, at 10.15 a.m. on April 25th 1945 - five years all but a month after I was first captured".

V.H. and I went on. It was afternoon and a scud of rain caught us as we regretfully said goodbye to D.T. and the others. We were allowed to shelter in the hospital yard, and persuaded the sister to take us up to see any wounded prisoners from the camp there might be, and were shown into a ward where there were five or six of them, all with leg amputations, all very cheerful in spite of obvious pain. They said they were being well looked after, with good food and some wine, brought in by civilians I gathered, and were interested to hear of our adventures and excited to know that the Americans were only two days off. One of them was Major Cousins of the escape over the wire; more numbering by the guards, and off we went.

It was an amusing party:- thirty five American enlisted men, just captured near Nurnberg, three Frenchmen captured in 1940, and two Russian Officers who were passing themselves off as "privates". The guards were 11 S.S. men, an old and faithful Sergeant Major who tried to carry out the advice of the Germans at the camp at Eichstätt to go slow and, maybe, meet the American forces in our company; a surly sergeant and a young officious private who was always ready to threaten the Sergeant Major if he treated us too easily. The Americans were very new to the prison game, and full of enthusiastic praise of a Scottish bombardier who had been with them up to date; he was a Dunkirk prisoner who had organised everything for them, somehow got Red Cross parcels and finally forged a doctor's signature to a chit which got him into Eichstätt hospital. As the Americans did not speak French, nor the French English, and only one of the party, besides the Russians, could speak German, it lacked natural cohesion, and V.H. and I had plenty to do in interpreting.

As we left Eichstätt, a straggling column with the luggage on a cart in front, we suddenly met a German we had talked to at Divisional Headquarters at Enslingen. "Where are the Americans?" we asked as usual. "Two hours behind" he said laughing. "Where are you off to?" "The Alps" he shouted, and went off down the road with a wave of his hand.

It was a short march that afternoon and, as was to be the programme for the next five days, at the end of the day's march our Sergeant Major went off to find somewhere for us to sleep. The village was full of S.S. Troops, the woods behind Eichstätt had more guns than we had seen previously, and forces seemed to have been brought up for the defence of the river. However, as always, the old man found us quite a comfortable barn, and with some vegetables and Red Cross food we had a good stew and a comfortable night.

    V.H. and I considered leaving the party that night. It was our last chance before the Danube when a stand might be made, but there were rumours that Stuttgart had been taken and so this possible line had already been outflanked. Besides this, the woods were obviously full of S.S. troops from whom we might get short shrift, and V.H. had some anxieties about his brother which could be resolved by a quiet march to Neuburg where the rest of the Eichstätt camp, we understood, was - the danger of being moved south as hostages to some Alpine redoubt seemed remote. So we decided against another flight, probably wisely as unpleasant rumours, we learnt afterwards, percolated through to Eichstätt about the treatment of escaped prisoners who were recaptured, We crossed the Danube at Neuburg the next day. One of the Americans had been hit by a careering tank the day before; he had been injured in the foot and could not walk, and we stopped at Neuburg to get him into hospital. It all took some time, and while we were in the main square the sirens went and planes came over; the calmest among us was a German nurse who took it all most philosophically She was a devout catholic and no Nazi, but her face became more than usually animated when we talked about Hitler in Berlin. "He has done right" she said, "he shows he is no coward to die fighting with his men". Then we left and three Americans and I carried the G.I. up to the hospital and with him came one named Tovey from the 1st Worcestershires, who had been lying up in a barn close by for some time, but had been driven by dysentery and hunger to come into Neuburg and give himself up. We got them to the hospital where the nurses took them in, showed us into a waiting room and gave us all coffee and rolls - and how Tovey ate - and allowed me to see some British and American patients in the hospital. On the way up we had passed the Fire Brigade standing to during the raid, one fireman with a short white beard and another with a big red face. This reminded me vividly of Tommy Walker and Dick Round of my days in the Stourbridge Fire Brigade, all complete as they were with brass helmets; I explained as I passed, in German, that at home I too had been in the fire brigade - nothing more. As we eventually made our way back the air raid was still on and the Brigade was still standing to but this time as we marched past they were called to attention and saluted me, as a veteran fireman. How proud I felt! Such is the camaraderie of the fire service.

Just south of the town there had been an aerodrome, and there we saw a sight for which we had in a way been waiting for so long - evidence of the effect of allied bombing. Here was devastation, wrecked buildings, tangled planes stretching for miles it seemed, and on the other side of the road enormous craters in the bare earth. Shortly afterwards we hit that night's billet, a barn set back in a farmyard. More stew; a talk with a Czech who had been drafted into the labour corps and told us that the aerodrome had been destroyed but the underground factory turning out jet planes was still intact; the discovery that in the straw on the top storey of the barn were some Russian escaped prisoners all added to the interest of the evening.

The guards were getting rather tired by this time. They said this was due to having to stay up and guard us by night and march by day. We did not think they need have worried about the guarding by night; they seemed to sleep soundly enough, and there was not much pretence made. However, on this night they decided to do it in style and had got beds for themselves in a kind of school dormitory across the road. Whether out of respect for officers, or fear of our inciting the others to walk out on them, they offered V.H. and me beds there too. We accepted, and were admitted into a room with an enormous fire, very welcome as the evening was a cold one, and one way and another we acquired and cooked an excellent meal, and then got to bed, V.H. and I on one side and the Germans on the other. It was interesting to notice that they did little more than take off their boots; for us it was a pleasure to get into pyjamas, or at any rate clean underclothes.

During a rather stuffy night - the windows did not open properly - a very young soldier toppled in through the door. He went up to V.H., the nearest of us to the door, and asked if he could take a bed. V.H. replied that he could, and not knowing we were English he told us he had been in such and such a division which had been "zersprengt", however being south of the Danube he was now out of the trap; exhausted but relieved he slumped down fully clothed to sleep. I wondered what this event, so early in his life, would have on him. This was one of the many incidents which reminded us of our own retreat from Belgium; continual withdrawal of troops; movement of refugees and anxious waiting by civilians; enemy planes searching by day; unconcerted desperate escaping of lost and exhausted troops by night.

On again through hopyards and townships and woodlands, trying always to find out where the Americans were, interrogating Italian and French prisoners and Poles as we made our way through, particularly when we stopped at midday for a meal. That evening, I think it was, we stopped in a barn, and while the old Feldwebel and I went off to get bread from the Major in charge of the bakery - much saluting and heel clicking on all sides here - V.H. had ingratiated himself with the farmer, with the result that we sat down to an enormous two course meal and a bottle of wine. It was a small boy who was our friend, completely captivated by some English Officers who had gone through not many days before, and ready to turn the place upside down for us. The chief aim on our part was to try to listen to the English news - we had arranged to sleep in the room where the apparatus was; unfortunately, however, the young German private, horrified at the prospect of our sleeping in better quarters than he, insisted on having one of the beds. And so we missed hearing the news again and elected to sleep in the barn with the rest of the men.

On again; eventually we reached Moosburg where there was a prison camp with a collection of over 40,000 British and American P.O.W. s together with large numbers or French, Dutch, Belgian, Russian and Yugoslavs - the population of a sizeable town. As we came into the camp we were split from other members of our party. It had been a very happy "Command". The young Scots Bombardier had warned me that the Americans would get in first on the rations if they could, leaving the Russians without food. Indeed at the first meal the Russians did not appear, apparently frightened to join the rest, and it took some persuasion to get them into the queue and we held up the distribution until they did. Afterwards all was well and the food was fairly divided. I was treated as the person in charge, resorted to for all sorts of things and with all sorts of problems. We had only been together for about 4 days, but we had built up quite a family feeling, and our farewells were tender. We wished the German Sergeant Major well for the future and gave him a chit praising him for a number of kindnesses he had shown to us on our march. The Russians were particularly warm in their farewells, with heartfelt hugs and thanks. I wonder what has happened to all of them. People come into one's life and then suddenly disappear and one can never expect to know any more about them; it is like some business which must for ever remain unfinished.

V.H. and I were put first of all into a room with 60 beds, inhabited by French, Dutch, Poles, Russians and Americans, and lice and bed bugs. Our human companions were all friendly, waiting for the war to end in a day or two's time. Next day we were transferred to the officers' compound, where we found our friends from Eichstätt already ensconced and well organised. On the following morning at an early hour we were told a strange story. The German Divisional Commander had asked the Americans that Moosburg should be treated as an open town, the chief argument being, of course, the very large P.O.W. Camp on its outskirts. The Americans agreed, provided that the Germans did not blow the bridges over the River Isar. This the German General would not accept. The German Kommandant, backed by the Senior British and American Officers, then went with the German Divisional General under a flag of truce to the American Divisional H.Q. to urge the proclamation of the town as "open". Again they were met with the same condition, but they then appealed to the American Corps Commander, with no better result. Negotiations at this stage were broken off and it was agreed that battle should commence at 0900 hours on the 29th April.

It seemed strange to us, as we waited for zero hour, that this procedure, reminiscent of the days of chivalry, could still be applied to that war. I doubt whether it could have happened in this way on the Eastern Front. Nine o'clock came and some American planes flew over the camp with a Victory Roll. A few bullets whistled around the camp, fired apparently in a private war between the German Army and the S.S. It was rumoured that the S.S. fired an anti tank weapon against army guards who said they were going to stay to guard us and not go and fight the Americans. We were told that three P.O.W.s were hurt in the fracas.

The bridge however remained unblown and there was no bombing of the town. In the course of the morning stars and stripes appeared in the town, and later various national flags in the camp. The German guards handed themselves in, so to speak, and soon after lunch a Sherman tank appeared on the Lagerstrasse and excitement started. But really there was little change in our condition, only that we provided our own guards. In so large a camp the wild joy of liberation rather passed us by. We hardly saw our liberators and everything was low key. It must have been quite different when a camp was quite small or one was on one's own; a prison friend of mine who was on the loose after leaving the march, walked into a village, saw the major and took the surrender of the population and its arms single handed before handing it all over to the Americans when they came up soon afterwards. That was much more memorable.

Two days later, on the 1st May I noted:

> "Today touched bottom. Probability of 7 days before starting evacuation; food shortage, terrible weather and darkness besides guard duty, no cooking and a very uncomfortable bed make liberation worse than imprisonment".

I was also suffering from diarrhoea, caused I expect by having drunk water from puddles and cart ruts while we were on the loose a week or so before.

The next day saw an improvement, with more food coming in, white bread - a gift from the American 3rd Army - and doughnuts from somewhere or another which ran out before I got one. We heard of terrible looting and stabbing by the Russians, natural in a way but most distasteful.

On the 3rd May we were told to stand by to leave, but nothing happened. On the 4th I went for a walk in the woods and a short peep at the town where things seemed more normal again, though looting continued. I met a young Pole in the camp who was rather a rogue, I expect, but delightful nonetheless, and we exchanged addresses; I thought I could perhaps be of help to him if he came to England as he thought he might. The news of the war was good, brought in by the radio; we found it hard, even then, to talk about the news more than in a whisper.

At 9.30 a.m. on the 7th May I was on the aerodrome at Landshut. The early and bumpy drive had not been comfortable. Forty to the lorry meant that we were standing up, not a good position when one had diarrhoea. But as I lay on the grass I could enjoy the warm sunshine and the blossom and the birdsong. The war seemed to have missed this part of Germany. So waiting for the planes was pleasant, a good thing as we were still there in the evening; we found some good billets nearby and I had a room to myself and a double bed. Things were looking up! On the 8th we returned to the airfield where there were some excitements; some sniping in woods nearby, and the sudden arrival of a plane with Nazi markings with the surrender of five occupants. Then at 7.15 we flew by Dakota to Rheims, and V.H. was able to listen to the King's Speech while in the air.

We were taken to an American reception centre for food and a camp bed and clean blankets. The reply to our thanks, "not at all sir, pleased to see you back", was heartening and heartfelt.

On the next day we drove around the town to avoid a service in the main square, by side streets under the Cathedral, with V signs and thrown kisses; back to the aerodrome, where we lay all day. At about 9.p.m. when many people had had nothing to eat all day, we were taken back through a drunk and cheering city to our billets, where we were fed. After about three and a half hours sleep we were up again and fed and taken back to the airfield, and after some wire pulling were embarked in a Lancaster for home. The crew had recently been dropping food to Holland, and dropping their own rations too. Looking back one is struck, and challenged, by the flood of goodness and kindness that bound us together in one ecstatic moment of almost universal goodwill.

We landed at Northolt aerodrome, and were taken to a reception centre at Chalfont St. Giles, with a reasonable dinner, fresh uniform throughout, a chance to telephone home and the first proper bath for 5 years. So, on the 10th May, five years to the day from Hitler's entry into Belgium - the start of the hot war - we came home.

There are two stories by way of epilogue to those five years. As I made my way by train to Birmingham from London I was spotted by a naval officer who concluded from my improvised rucksack that I was an old prisoner. He had been back some weeks from a Marlag and when I asked what things were like he said "marvellous. There is as much bread as you can eat and it tastes like cake".

The next incident takes us further forward in time. I have referred to the Pole whom I met in Moosburg and with whom I exchanged addresses. Some time after I returned home I received a letter from him, in German which was the language in which we had spoken in the camp. He said he was still in Germany, and added, "My young life is in danger". It appeared that he had a kidney infection, for which a doctor had prescribed penicillin, but this did not exist in Germany; could I let him have any? I enquired from chemists and doctors, but chemists could not provide this without a prescription from a British doctor, and no doctor could prescribe without seeing the patient. I was advised to send vitamin tablets which I did. Later I heard of his return to

Poland, and then I had a letter from his brother who said he was very ill, and could I send him a suit of clothes. This was in the days of clothes rationing. So armed with coupons I went to Lewis's in Birmingham and bought a suit off the peg of what I hoped was a sensible size and sent it out to him. Some time later I heard he had died, and later still I had a photograph of him lying in state, looking very peaceful, with all his family around him, dressed in my suit. I have felt that no gift could have been more valuable to the family, whose honour had been maintained in his death
and this final record of their sorrow and pride.

    Five years of one's life spent in the way I have described would appear to be a waste of opportunities and experiences. Yet, though such a fate would never be sought, it did, I believe, have rare compensations. I learnt, I hope, that we have reserves beyond anything that we can imagine; that material things are of small value and not in themselves worth the struggle of acquiring or holding, and that being attached to things means being controlled by them; that on the other hand hunger saps one's character in a way that it is hard to credit in times of plenty; that above all, the only important thing in life is relationships with one's fellows and all around one, hard indeed though they are to maintain. I was blessed beyond desert in my friends, many of whom I still see and whose companionship is as easy as when I last saw them. I think I learnt more from this period of my life than from any other; things work out in unexpected and surprisingly beneficial ways if one can let them.

****

Pictures added by Jane Stanley (neé Evers)

Bryan Evers age 21

Stourbridge Voluntary Fire Brigade c.1939

Top row: Denis Evers 2nd from left, Bryan 4th from left, John Green far right

125

2nd Lieutenant B G Evers
Service number: 89661
Royal Artillery

Birmingham Daily Gazette
Friday 26th July 1940

Peer's Heir a Prisoner

The Earl and Countess of Ellesmere have received news from a private neutral source that Viscount Brackley, their only son, aged 25, a second lieutenant, who has been missing since 6 June, is a prisoner of war. Last year he married Lady Diana Percy, whose brother, the Duke of Northumberland, was recently killed in action.

Mr. W. O. Taylor, a Leamington teacher, has received news that his son is a prisoner of war.

There is, from inquiries made by his family, reason to believe that Captain G. Evers, son of Mr. F. P. Evers, North Worcestershire Coroner, was killed in action on 29 May.

Rugby Advertiser
Friday 17th October 1941

CRICKET IN GERMAN PRISON CAMPS

RUGBY v. MARLBOROUGH

"LETTERS home from Capt. G. Evern (O.R., Cotton) and 2nd.-Lieut. D. C. Preston (O.R., Cotton), of the Green Howards, both prisoners of war in Oflag VB," says "The Meteor," "state that on Thursday, July 31st, a cricket match, with stools as wickets and a tennis ball, was played in the camp between representatives of Rugby and Marlborough, ending in a victory for Rugby by 57 runs to 33. At a 'dinner' the same evening the following O.R's. were present: N. A. Pattullo (Tudor, 1915-1920), M. Greenwood (Dickinson, 1922-1926), M. Sturton (S.H., 1934-1937), J. Gordon (School Field, 1930-1934), A. S. T. Young (H.J.H., 1932-1936), M. H. A. Martin (Stanley, 1924-1929)."

Rugby Advertiser
Friday 25th October 1940

Old Rugbeians In The War

CASUALTIES AND HONOURS

THE Meteor announces that to date 32 Old Rugbeians have been killed in the war, 16 wounded, 22 are prisoners, and 9 are missing.

Latest additions to the list of those who have been killed are:— Wing-Commander E. C. Barlow, R.A.F. (School Field), Second-Lieut. R. D. Delsham, Royal Artillery (Dickinson), Second-Lieut. M. K. St Hill, Royal Fusiliers (Michell), Lieut. J. W. Shairp, C.A., Ayrshire Yeomanry (Whitelaw), Squadron-Leader N. W. Wadham, R.A.F. (School Field), Lieut. P. T. Eckersley, M.P., Royal Naval Volunteer Reserve (School Field), Flying Officer E. A. Beale, R.A.F. (Cotton), Lieut. (Acting Captain) P. J. Fulton, Lancashire Fusiliers (Tudor), Second-Lieut. S. W. G. Bingay, Royal Berkshire Regiment (School House).

The following are prisoners of war: Capt. A. H. Foa, Hussars (Whitelaw), Capt. G. Evers, Royal Artillery (Cotton), Capt. H. L. Pumfrett, Royal Army Service Corps (Tudor), Second-Lieut. J. N. V. A. Lemieux, Royal Hussars (Stanley), Capt. C. J. E. Yeo, Royal Artillery (Kilbracken), Capt. E. H. Lynn Allen, Gloucestershire Regi-

Kriegsgefangenenpost

Postkarte

PASSED
P.W. 3270

Gebührenfrei!

Absender:
Vor- und Zuname: CAPT. B. EVERS
Gefangenennummer: 1561
Lager-Bezeichnung: VII B
Deutschland (Allemagne)

Empfangsort: MRS. G.V. EVERS
ROCK MOUNT
NR. STOURBRIDGE
Straße: WORCESTERSHIRE
Land: ENGLAND
Landesteil (Provinz usw.)

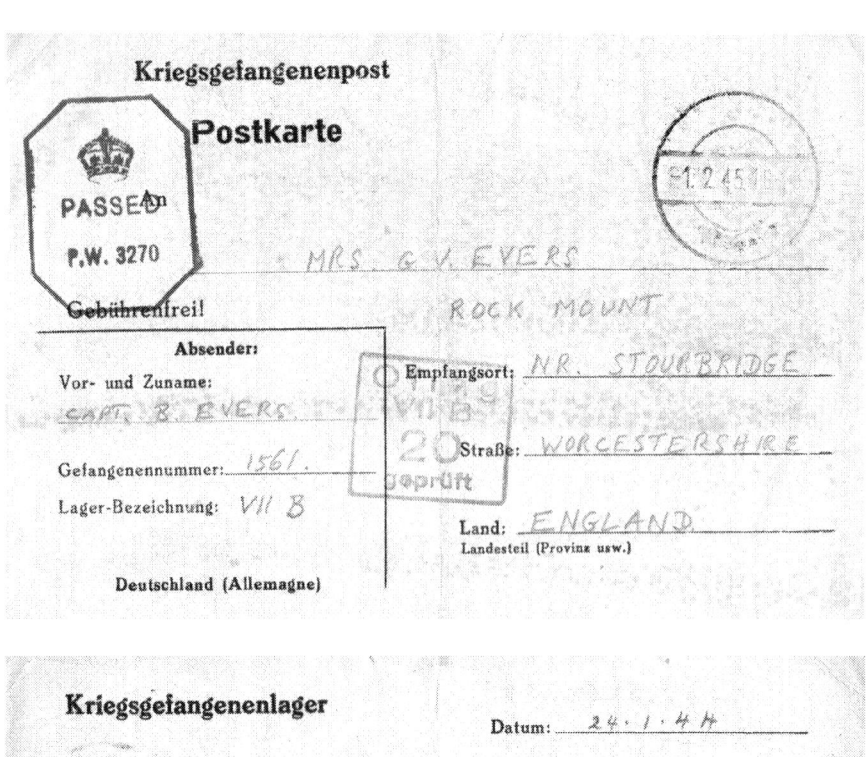

Kriegsgefangenenlager

Datum: 24.1.44

Having had no letters for ages & nobody particular to write to, so here is a friendly one. Skating which was in full swing, has given way to snow, which is rather heavy & depressing. However a new batch of Arnhem prisoners has provided us with new ideas & thoughts, & hopes for new friends. Spring should cheer you too soon. Love to you & everyone.

Postcard to his uncle and aunt, Guy and Kathleen Evers

Kriegsgefangenenpost

Postkarte

An R. D. M. EVERS ESQ
ROCK MOUNT,
Empfangsort: NR STOURBRIDGE
Straße: WORCESTERSHIRE
Land: ENGLAND

Absender:
Vor- und Zuname: CAPT R EVERS
Gefangenennummer: 1561
Lager-Bezeichnung: Kriegsgef.-Offizierlager VII B
Deutschland (Allemagne)

PASSED P.W. 3270
15.10.44

Kriegsgefangenenlager

Datum: 9·10·44

I get occasional news of you & your doings, but cannot well picture them, & the same applies to Ruth. I keep meeting friends & acquaintances of yours; the last is a Canadian named Bill who played against you at cricket on your Vandals tour. I am doing some law with Dick Trafford who, having done very well in his Bar exam, is going in for a scholarship. Sounds peaceful & academic doesn't it? Best wishes to you, as always
Bill.

Postcard to his cousin Denis Evers RAF

Eichstätt Oflag VII-B POW camp for Officers,
60 miles north of Munich.

Bryan's photo of winter ice skating at Oflag VII B

Bryan's photo of a boxing match at Oflag VII B

Bryan (POW no. 1561) standing, second from left

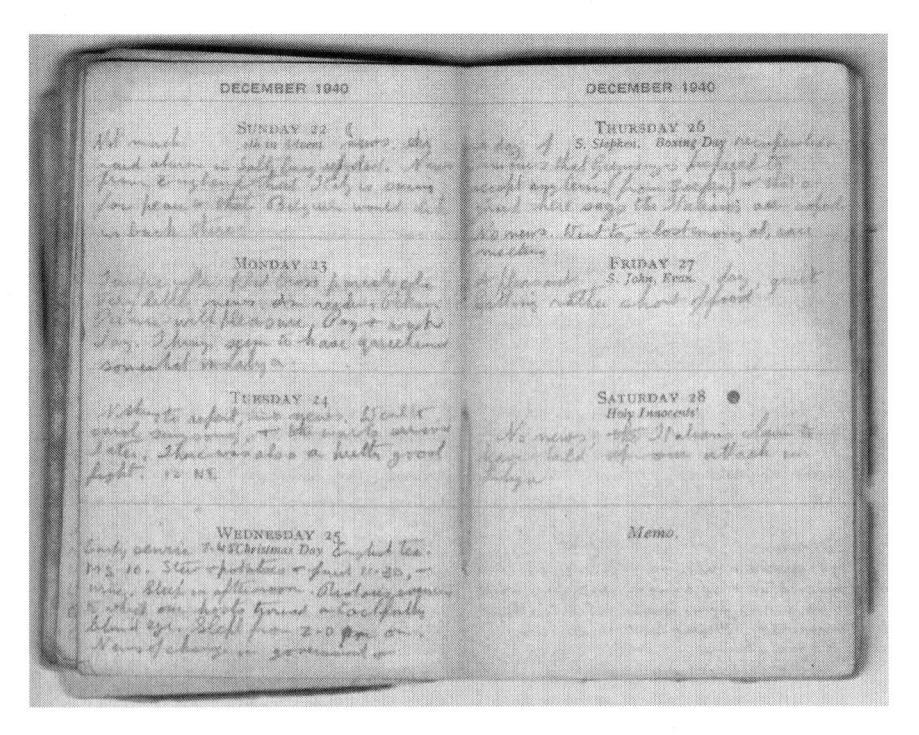

Bryan's diary (70mm x 100mm) – first Christmas in captivity

Numb. 37368

SUPPLEMENT
TO
The London Gazette
Of TUESDAY, the 27th of NOVEMBER, 1945
Published by Authority

Registered as a newspaper

THURSDAY, 29 NOVEMBER, 1945

CENTRAL CHANCERY OF THE ORDERS
OF KNIGHTHOOD.

St. James's Palace, S.W.1.
29th November, 1945.

The KING has been graciously pleased to give orders for the following appointments to the Most Excellent Order of the British Empire, in recognition of gallant and distinguished services in the field:—

To be Additional Members of the Military Division of the said Most Excellent Order:—

No. 2074 Warrant Officer Class I Lestock Ryvers BAIGENT, New Zealand Military Forces.
No. 5485467 Warrant Officer Class I Joseph Edward EAMES, The Royal Sussex Regiment.
Major (temporary) Miles Belfrage REID, M.C. (119433), General List (Midhurst, Sussex).
Lieutenant Christopher Gorham STURT (120611), Royal Army Pay Corps (Radlett, Herts.).

(The ranks shown against the names of the Officers are those held by them at the time they were recommended.)

CENTRAL CHANCERY OF THE ORDERS
OF KNIGHTHOOD.

St. James's Palace, S.W.1.
29th November, 1945.

The KING has been graciously pleased to approve the award of the British Empire Medal (Military Division), in recognition of gallant and distinguished services in Burma, to the undermentioned:—

No. 18900 Regimental Sergeant-Major ALI HERSI, The King's African Rifles.
No. 2012961 Sapper Richard Edward HARMAN, Corps of Royal Engineers (St. Leonards-on-Sea).
No. 1893140 Sergeant Richard Metcalfe IVESON, Corps of Royal Engineers (Shipley, Yorks.).
No. 101307 Mechanist Staff-Sergeant Robert Gordon KENNINGTON, East Africa Electrical and Mechanical Engineers.
No. 4982644 Sergeant (acting) Victor Lawrence REEVES, Intelligence Corps (London, N.W.10.).
No. SLA/36019 Regimental Sergeant-Major TAMBA BAIMA, The Sierra Leone Regiment (Royal West African Frontier Force).

War Office, 29th November, 1945.

The KING has been graciously pleased to approve the following awards in recognition of gallant and distinguished services in the field:—

Bar to the Military Cross.

Captain (temporary) John Murray ANDERSON, M.C. (90084), The Seaforth Highlanders (Ross-shire Buffs, The Duke of Albany's) (East Grinstead).

The Military Cross.

Lieutenant Peter Richard Beverley BOTES (255230), Royal Armoured Corps (Kingston-on-Thames).
Major (temporary) Richard William ROGERSON (7354), Royal Regiment of Artillery (Richmond, Yorks).
Captain (temporary) Bryan Grosvenor EVERS (89661), Royal Regiment of Artillery (Stourbridge). ←
Captain (temporary) Francis Paul KEYSELL (113170), Royal Regiment of Artillery (Stevenage, Kent).
Lieutenant John Rollo BARRETT (78447), Royal Regiment of Artillery (Hedden-on-the-Wall).
Lieutenant Kenneth Harry ROSCOE (66953), Corps of Royal Engineers (Stoke-on-Trent).
Captain (temporary) Archibald Charles William NOEL (62578), Welsh Guards (Dundee).
Second-Lieutenant Hamish Stewart FORBES (72465), Welsh Guards (London, S.W.6).
Captain (temporary) James BRUCE (67100), The Royal Scots (The Royal Regiment) (Camberley).
Major (temporary) Erracht Pryce Cameron BRUCE (31881), The Buffs (Royal East Kent Regiment) (Sherbourne, Dorset).
Captain (temporary) Ernest Lorne Campbell EDLMANN (63568), The Buffs (Royal East Kent Regiment) (Cheltenham).
Captain (temporary) Robert Owen Forsyth PRICHARD (64603), The Royal Welch Fusiliers (Farnham, Surrey).
Lieutenant Robert Mark CARPENTER (92334), The South Wales Borderers (Gateshead-on-Tyne).
Captain (acting) Charles Hughlings JACKSON (38234), The Royal Sussex Regiment (Guildford, Surrey).
Lieutenant Brian Cheveley PHILLIPS (121209), The Queen's Own Royal West Kent Regiment.
Lieutenant Peter David Stone PUGH (98777), The Queen's Own Royal West Kent Regiment (Sevenoaks).
Lieutenant Arnold John WATERS (105482), The Queen's Own Royal West Kent Regiment (Sevenoaks).
Captain (temporary) Peter John BLUNDELL (86471), The King's Royal Rifle Corps (Northwood, Middx).
Lieutenant Nicholas John WARRY (217620), The King's Royal Rifle Corps (Yeovil).
Lieutenant David Grey WORCESTER (232585), Special Air Service Regiment, Army Air Corps (Aberystwyth).
Captain Alexander Robert Taylor LUNDIE, M.B. (94926), Royal Army Medical Corps (Cupar).
Captain (temporary) Henry Rogers TURNER (318 A1), Indian Armoured Corps.
Jemadar CHAIN SINGH, Indian Armoured Corps.
Captain Edward Stirling RIVETT-CARNAC (8793 V), South African Forces.

SUPPLEMENT TO THE LONDON GAZETTE, 31 JANUARY, 1946

To be Additional Associates of the Royal Red Cross, Second Class:—

Sister Blanche HELLIWELL (50763), New Zealand Army Nursing Service.
Sister Amy Marion Baxter KERR (42287), New Zealand Army Nursing Service.

The Military Medal.

No. 854739 Sergeant Cyril Victor BENSLEY, Royal Horse Artillery.
No. 7911803 Trooper William Denton VENABLES, 4th Queen's Own Hussars, Royal Armoured Corps.
No. 913565 Lance-Sergeant Harry SWAINBANK, Royal Regiment of Artillery.
No. 1888304 Lance-Corporal Robert Brimer WATSON, Corps of Royal Engineers.
No. 2320992 Sergeant Reginald Harold EVERSON, Royal Corps of Signals.
No. 2572226 Signalman Leonard Edward CAMPLIN, Royal Corps of Signals.
No. 1793157 Private Arthur Raymond WEBBER, The Royal Scots (The Royal Regiment).
No. 5111697 Private Beverley Stephens HEWITT, The Royal Warwickshire Regiment.
No. 4192770 Fusilier John EVANS, The Royal Welch Fusiliers.
No. 6666187 Private Edward George RANKMORE, The Seaforth Highlanders (Ross-shire Buffs, The Duke of Albany's).
No. 2820354 Private John William WILSON, The Seaforth Highlanders (Ross-shire Buffs, The Duke of Albany's).
No. 2751171 Sergeant Thomas GLASSEY, The Argyll and Sutherland Highlanders (Princess Louise's).
No. 3909446 Trooper Anthony MERRYWEATHER, Army Air Corps.
No. 2338543 Private Derek WARREN, Royal Electrical and Mechanical Engineers.
No. 34361 Sapper Noel Edwin ANDREWS, New Zealand Military Forces.
No. 62457 Private Arthur Wallace SCOTT, New Zealand Military Forces.
No. Pal.12146 Private Rachmiel SKURNICKI, Palestine Regiment.

War Office, 31st January, 1946.

The KING has been graciously pleased to approve that the following be Mentioned in recognition of gallant and distinguished services in the field:—

Royal Armoured Corps.
788442 Sergt. E. CHAPMAN.

R.T.R.
Lt. R. H. C. EASTMAN (73367).
Lt. R. J. SAGE (189823).
7890052 Tpr. L. L. THOMAS.

1st E. Riding Yeo.
Maj H. M. V. WRIGHT, D.S.O., T.D. (33615).

Yorkshire Hussars.
6141160 Tpr. A. J. MURPHY.

Royal Regiment of Artillery.
Capt. A. W. LISTER (71023).
Capt. H. WESTLEY (7363).
Capt. (temp.) B. G. EVERS, M.C. (89661).
Lt. P. R. EVANS (90446).
1469258 Sergt. S. MILLING.
1480185 Bdr. W. J. OSBOND.
891679 Lce.-Bdr. C. A. HOGAN.
842956 Lce.-Bdr. C. F. RIDLEY.
851712 Gnr. C. COLLINS.
891716 Gnr. J. E. HOGAN.

Corps of Royal Engineers.
Maj. G. WHITEHEAD (35709).
Maj. (temp.) I. C. C. MACKENZIE (109400).
Capt. (temp.) A. D. SIMMONS (136907).
Lt. J. S. BARKER (125190).
2181955 W.O. I (actg.) J. CAIRNS.
1986704 W.O. II (actg.) B. HAMER.
1875793 W.O. II (actg.) S. R. WYATT.

Royal Corps of Signals.
2328063 Lce.-Cpl. E. GRIMMANT.

Foot Guards.
W. G'ds.
2735135 Gdsmn. D. R. KEAY.

Infantry.

The Queen's R.
Capt. A. C. MacE. SAVAGE (63567).
6090480 Pte. N. C. BAKER.

The Buffs.
6284696 Sergt. C. R. McKAY, M.M.
6284203 Pte. R. J. EDWARDS.
6286396 Pte. A. MANSER.

R. North'd Fus.
Lt. T. H. ELLIOTT (74118).
4447084 Sergt. J. R. STODDART.

R. War. R.
5110851 Pte. J. WILD.

R.W. Fus.
Maj. D. I. OWEN (14234).

Cheshire R.
4129110 Cpl. G. J. POOLE.

Worc. R.
Capt. D. B. HASLEHUST (77638).
Lt. R. A. WEEKS (89338).

D.W.R.
4616375 Lce.-Sgt. D. BEVERLEY.

Border R.
Lt. J. TURNBULL, M.C. (76078).

Black Watch.
Capt. (temp.) G. I. A. DUNCAN, M.C. (132481).

Oxf. & Bucks. L.I.
5384465 Sergt. J. P. LINGANE.

R.W.K.
Lt. I. B. MACASKIE (86215).

K.O.Y.L.I.
4690724 Pte. A. TURNER.

Y. & L.R.
4748858 Pte. L. BINNS.

Durham L.I.
Maj. (temp.) G. M. NORMAN (156759).

Seaforth.
Maj. R. F. NASON (6256).
3058496 Pte. J. ROBSON.

Camerons.
Capt. (temp.) A. M. ALLAN (117901).
2924265 W.O.I (actg.) C. MACKINTOSH, M.C.

A. & S.H.
Maj. R. M. YOUNG (31340).

Royal Army Service Corps.
CY.82 Sergt. A. JACOVIDES.
CY.69 Dvr. N. COSTE.
94762 Pte. G. D. SCOTLAND.
S/3913033 Pte. D. J. THOMAS.

Royal Army Medical Corps.
Maj. (temp.) R. MACKAY, M.C., M.D. (139329).
Capt. A. H. WESTON, M.B. (41716).
Capt. J. E. WOODING (107205).

The Cyprus Regiment.
CY.2307 Pte. G. A. FRANTZIS.
Pte. Mustapha Achmet PECRI.

Pioneer Corps.
Capt. (temp.) H. E. G. RAYMENT (132356).

Intelligence Corps.
2888477 Sergt. J. EDGAR.

General List.
Maj. H. J. FRAGER (305088).
Lt. P. J. AMPHLETT (270979).

INDIAN ARMY.

Indian Armoured Corps.
8 Lt. Cav.
Col. M. C. WADDILOVE, O.B.E. (IA.994).

Indian Medical Service.
Capt. P. R. DAS-GUPTA, M.B. (MZ.20717).

New Zealand Military Forces.
Maj. H. A. A. STEVELY (50008).
Capt. J. A. ALLEN (60295).

Coroner 1947 - 1982

Uncle B in his Morris Minor

The Cypress Leylandii dedicated to Bryan by Stourbridge Rotary Club in 2009. It was planted on Rotary Ridge at the National Memorial Arboretum, Staffordshire.

Acknowledgements

Once again my huge thanks go to Ian Henderson without whom I could not have got this book ready to be re-published. I am eternally grateful Ian.

My thanks also go to:

Michael Evers for writing the Foreword.

Colonel Stamford Cartwright, Honorary Curator of the Worcestershire Yeomanry Museum Collection and a very good friend of Bryan's, for his invaluable help.

Andrea Denby, genealogist, for researching the articles on pages 127, 131 and 132.

Sharon Caldwell of the Worcestershire Coroners' Court for the picture of Bryan.

Kirstin Dodd of the National Memorial Museum in Staffordshire for the pictures of the plaque and tree dedicated to Bryan by the Stourbridge Rotary Club in 2009.